# KYLE NEWSOME

FOREWORD BY: L. SHAWADEIM REAGANS

**I BEFORE E:**

**Influence and Impact Lead to Long-Term Effectiveness. Forget About Control.**



Published by Mental Tech Publishing

Foreword by L. Shawadeim Reagans

## EDUCATIONAL DISCLAIMER

This book is intended for educational purposes and reflects the author's experiences and perspectives on leadership and mentorship. It is not professional advice.

Some names and identifying details have been changed to protect privacy. Any resemblance to actual persons or events is coincidental.

ISBN: 979-8-9950912-0-2

First Edition

Printed in the United States of America

Artwork and Design by: Next Level Publishing

To request media appearances, book speaking engagements, or place book orders, please contact us at info@KNewsome.com

**Foreword by L. Shawadeim Reagans**

It is said, "We do not learn from experiences; we learn from reflecting on experiences." In that spirit, while there is a privilege in growing older, age alone does not make one wise.

This book is not written from a position of power, nor from a stage looking down. It is not about speaking to the powerless. These reflections come from an empowered leader, one who has leveraged a lifetime of experiences to show up for young people consistently and intentionally so that they, too, can be empowered.

When Ol' Dirty Bastard stormed the Grammy stage in frustration and disbelief over his group being overlooked, he reminded the world that "Wu-Tang is for the children... We teach the babies." Whether or not you agree with, or even fully understand what ODB meant, know this: Kyle Newsome is for the children. He teaches the babies.

This book was written to reach you, because committing to young people requires more than intention. It takes both head-work and heart-work. There are no magic formulas, only an unwavering commitment.

Kyle Newsome, aka New, shares from an authentic place. The place where titles do not matter, but presence does. Although he marks 1992 as the start of his professional journey, the wisdom in these pages is drawn from lived experiences that precede that year. He offers reflections on missteps and breakthroughs, on connection and correction, on how we show up when control is an illusion, and all we have left is influence. Real, earned influence is where everything begins. Wins and lessons.

New does not offer perfection but perspective: hard-earned, heart-driven perspective from someone who has walked alongside kids navigating systems not designed to see them, but to control them. The same systems that did not see him. He has learned, sometimes the hard way, that control does not bring about impactful change.

So, let us reflect and reframe how we lead, teach, and reach. When young people trust your presence, they make space for your influence. When they see your authenticity, they start to believe in their own. Whether you are a teacher teetering on the edge of burnout or feeling as energized as a wide-eyed new educator before the start of the school year; whether you are in a formal leadership role tasked with inspiring others to prove what is possible; or whether you are a mentor, counselor, coach, caregiver, parent, or advocate; this book was written with you in mind.

Embrace the reflections, questions, challenges, and reminders. Use the tools, adapt them, apply them, or simply sit with them. Let us begin with care, not with strategies, but with self-awareness. Let us teach young people not only how to behave, but how to positively contribute to their becoming.

*THIS BOOK IS FOR THOSE WHO SHOW UP FOR CHILDREN EVERY DAY.*

# TABLE OF CONTENTS

MESSAGE FROM THE AUTHOR:

# FROM EXPERIENCE TO INSIGHT: MY WHY

## WHY DID I WRITE THIS BOOK?

That question, while seemingly simple, has been a deeply reflective one for me. I've dedicated my professional life to working with children since 1992. Over the past three decades, I have had the privilege of engaging with youth in a diverse range of settings, including classrooms, residential treatment facilities, behavioral programs, community mentoring initiatives, and public forums. Whether speaking at a podium or working one-on-one with a student in crisis, my journey has been defined by a consistent and urgent question: *How do we reach young people where they are, and help guide them to where they can be?*

My experience spans a broad spectrum of educational and youth service institutions, including Youth Consultation Services, the Board of Education, and KIPP Charter Schools, among others. These institutions have afforded me a front-row seat to both the triumphs and challenges inherent in youth engagement. And yet, despite the years and titles, I remain a student. I'm constantly learning from each encounter, every success, and yes, every misstep.

This book is a personal reflection on decades of working with youth, highlighting real-life experiences in education, mentoring, and behavioral intervention. It is not an absolute authority, nor does it pretend to offer a one-size-fits-all solution. Rather, it is a collection of lessons learned through trial, error, and growth; lessons that have shaped how I view youth development and how I engage with young people across a range of circumstances.

*"This isn't a rulebook. It's a reflection, a relationship, a reminder."*

It is a testimony. Let me be clear: this book is not a definitive manual, nor does it claim to be the final word on how to reach and teach today's youth. The world is evolving, and so too are our students. What I offer here are insights and tools and strategies born of practical experience, shaped by reflection, and grounded in authentic human connection. Some of these insights may affirm what you are already doing well. Others may challenge you to rethink your approach, and perhaps some may simply give you the pause to reflect on your role, your methods, and your mission.

I hope that this book will serve as both a mirror and a compass: a mirror to reflect on your current practice, and a compass to guide you toward deeper, more effective engagement with the young people you serve. Whether you are an educator, parent, coach, mentor, counselor, or advocate, you have a vital role in shaping the next generation. I aim to support you in that work; to help you become not just better, but sharper, more intentional, and more impactful with every interaction.

Let us begin.

INTRODUCTION

# I BEFORE E: INFLUENCE BEFORE EFFECTIVENESS (AND FORGET ABOUT CONTROL)

As educators, our mission transcends the mere imparting of knowledge; we aim to ignite a passion for learning and inspire meaningful change. Today, I want to share with you a transformative concept that can redefine how we approach teaching: the "I Before E" philosophy.

Traditionally, "I before E, except after C" is a mnemonic rule of thumb for English spelling. If you're unsure whether a word is spelled with *ei* or *ie,* the rhyme suggests the correct order is *ie* unless the preceding letter is c, in which case it may be *ei*. That's how most of us learned it in school. But in this book, I, E, and C each take on a different, much deeper meaning.

Here, ***I*** stands for Influence, ***E*** for Effectiveness, and ***C*** for Control. And just like in the spelling rule, there's a catch when C shows up first. When control leads the way, coming before influence, it tends to distort everything that follows. Control is an overused and often unsuccessful approach to engaging with children of any age. It's rooted in fear, reinforced by white supremacy culture, propped up by extrinsic motivation, and it often delivers nothing more than temporary compliance.

That's why I propose we flip the traditional formula. Influence must come before effectiveness and control. Control doesn't belong in the equation. If we want to reach young people in real, transformative ways, we have to prioritize connection over compliance, and presence over power. Let's forget about the ***C***, and focus on what truly matters: showing up with influence, so that real effectiveness can follow.

## FROM THE CLASSROOM, TO THE COURTROOM, TO THE CORNER

Let me take you back to where it all started for me. I didn't start this journey with a grand plan or a perfect blueprint. I started with a moment. My first time working with youth was more than a lesson in teaching; it was a crash course in life. It was messy, unpredictable, and deeply human. I wasn't in a fancy classroom with a shiny whiteboard or a textbook. No, I was on the front lines, doing whatever I could to connect with young people who were skeptical of any adult claiming to "help" them. I remember standing in a gym full of middle schoolers. I was fresh out of college, nervous, but trying to look confident.

A kid with baggy jeans and a skeptical stare asked, "You really here to help, or are you just getting a paycheck?"

That question stuck with me. It was my first real day working with youth, and I had no idea what I was doing. But in that moment, I knew this was going to be more than a job. It was the start of a journey that would take me from the classroom to the courtroom, to the corner store, and back again.

In this journey of over thirty years, I've worked in all kinds of spaces: public schools, behavioral programs, court-involved youth settings, mentoring programs, and residential facilities. I've seen brilliance hidden beneath behavioral write-ups. I've seen systems break young people, and young people who have learned to survive by breaking the rules. I've sat across from young people who were just one bad decision away from losing everything, and I've seen the same young people transform before my eyes when they felt seen, heard, and cared for.

But here's the thing: these young people raised me as much as I tried to raise them. The growth was mutual. The lessons were just as much mine as theirs. Whether I was in a classroom, a courtroom, or a corner store, what I learned from them was always more profound than what I could teach them. Each space and each interaction was a chance for me to evolve and to stop thinking of myself as the "expert" and start seeing myself as a fellow human being on a shared journey.

That journey has taught me that real teaching isn't about having all the answers. It's about showing up, staying present, and learning together.

## NOT A GURU | JUST A GROWN-UP WHO CARES

Before we dive deep, let me be clear: I'm not here as a guru. I'm not writing this book as someone who's figured it all out. This isn't coming from the mountaintop. It's coming from the hallway outside the principal's office; from a cafeteria full of noise and possibility; from the back row of a courtroom where a student waits to hear their fate; from the front seat of a van taking a kid home who just got suspended... again. I've had lessons blow up in my face. I've learned the hard way. I've made my share of mistakes, missed the mark, misread a moment, and mishandled situations I should have approached with more patience or more understanding. I'm still learning. Still growing. Still getting checked by a thirteen-year-old with a hoodie and headphones.

This work isn't about perfection. It's about progress. It's about presence. And most of all, it's about care. The goal isn't to present a one-size-fits-all guide to fixing youth. This book is a mirror, not a manual. It's a call to reflect on yourself, on your practice, and on the bigger picture.

## CONTROL IS COMFORTING, BUT IT RARELY WORKS

Control feels safe. Predictable. It gives us the illusion that if we can just tighten our grip on behavior, on schedules, or on outcomes, everything will stay in order. But in real life, especially when working with young people navigating trauma, distrust, or survival mode, control rarely delivers what it promises.

I've learned, sometimes the hard way, that control is often rooted not in strength, but in fear. Fear of chaos. Fear of failure. Fear of being vulnerable in front of the very young people we're trying to lead. But fear doesn't build relationships. It doesn't create safety, and it sure does not create trust. What it often creates instead is resistance, rebellion, or silence.

"I Before E" flips the script. It reminds us to put Influence before Effectiveness, and to forget about Control. Not because structure and boundaries don't matter, they absolutely do, but because control as a mindset, as a posture, is often more about us than it is about them. It's about our comfort, our authority, our desire to avoid the messiness of real connection.

But influence? Influence is different. Influence is rooted in trust, presence, and connection. It can't be demanded. It is earned. It grows slowly, through consistent actions and authentic relationships. Influence means showing up, again and again, even when it's hard. It means listening more than lecturing. It means letting go of being right to do what's real.

When you prioritize influence, everything begins to shift. The classroom, or program, or corner, is no longer about power dynamics; it's about partnership. You stop trying to manage behavior and start nurturing growth. You stop clinging to rigid rules and start creating meaningful expectations grounded in mutual respect.

And here's the powerful truth: when students feel your influence, when they trust your presence, effectiveness follows. Not the kind you can always measure on a chart or a test, but the kind that shows up in eye contact, in effort, in the quiet moment when a young person lets their guard down just enough to let you in.

Letting go of control doesn't mean letting go of accountability. It means choosing a deeper kind of leadership. One that trades fear for faith. Ego for empathy. Systems of dominance for systems of care.

So yes, control may feel comforting. But it rarely works. Influence though? Influence transforms.

## YOUNG PEOPLE ARE DIFFERENT | BUT SO ARE WE

Today's youth are louder, faster, more aware, and more overwhelmed. They're growing up in a world where information moves at the speed of a scroll, and so do opinions, identities, and insecurities. TikTok trends shape culture overnight. Trauma is no longer tucked away; it's trending. Tests measure more than just academic growth; they measure endurance. And triggers? They're everywhere. Young people nowadays are navigating a digital and emotional landscape we never had to at their age.

But here's the thing: while young people are evolving, so must we. We can't keep showing up with chalkboard mindsets in a touchscreen world. The old-school rules we once relied on, silent hallways, one-size-fits-all discipline, rigid hierarchies, don't resonate with new-school minds. It isn't just "young people these days." These young people are mirrors of a society that's speeding up and spiraling in new ways.

They need educators who can decode the difference between defiance and distress, who can see past the hoodie, the Beats, the Air Pods, or the eye roll, and respond with curiosity instead of control. They need new tools; tools built on empathy, adaptability, and cultural awareness.

And let's be real, we are different too. We carry more awareness, more access, and hopefully more humility than we once did. We've been challenged, checked, and changed by the work. This moment isn't just asking us to teach, it's asking us to transform.

If we don't adjust, we risk losing the very connection we're striving for. But if we evolve alongside them, we have a shot at not just reaching today's youth, but also walking with them into a future we can shape together.

## WHAT IF YOU'RE THE LESSON?

Let's flip the lens for a moment. What if the most powerful lesson in your classroom isn't just what's written on the whiteboard or syllabus, but how you show up every day? You might be the biggest curriculum your students experience this year. Long before they absorb the content, they're watching you, how you talk when frustrated, how you move when rushed, how you respond when challenged, disrespected, or wrong. Every sigh, smile, and moment of vulnerability or strength is a page in the lesson they're unconsciously and quietly reading.

In a world flooded with mixed messages and divided narratives, the most authentic lesson is often not *what* we say, but what we *do*. Young people are craving authenticity. They do not just need facts. They need to see what grace looks like when it's needed, what accountability feels like when it's earned, and what growth sounds like when it stumbles before it soars. Young people aren't just asking, "What are you teaching me?" They're wondering, "Can I trust you?" Your presence speaks volumes. Your values are on display, not in a syllabus, but in how you treat the student who struggles, the one who acts out, or the one who reminds you of your younger self.

Ask yourself: Are you just giving a lecture, or offering a real-life lesson in how to show up, care, and be present? Are you the test or the testimony?

Young people don't just need content. They need a consistent example. Are you the lesson they'll carry with them? Are you modeling the values you want them to embody? Every day, every interaction is an opportunity to teach not just with words, but with your example.

You are the test, the testimony, and the transformation. Every day, you're either reinforcing the lesson or rewriting it. The most unforgettable lessons are the ones they experience, not just the ones they hear. Every interaction with your students is an opportunity to teach through both content and character.

## THIS BOOK IS A MIRROR, NOT A MANUAL

This isn't a manual. It's a mirror. You won't find formulas, quick-fix strategies, or a one-size-fits-all blueprint in these pages. What you will find are reflections, stories, hard truths, and maybe even a few moments that make you uncomfortable. That's by design. The work we do as educators and mentors is not linear, it's layered. It's messy. It's deeply human. And it doesn't start with policy or procedure. It starts with presence.

This book isn't here to hand you rules; it's here to hold up a mirror. Not to point fingers, but to invite reflection. It is intended to get you to look inward before trying to lay down the law outward. To pause and ask, who am *I* in the room with these young people? What am I modeling when no one's watching?

This is an invitation to think differently, to move differently, to show up real. Not polished. Not perfect. Just present. Because what if the most transformative thing in your classroom isn't a lesson plan or a new strategy, but you? Your values. Your consistency. Your willingness to be seen.

You are the curriculum. You are the standard. You are the influence. So before we reach for solutions, let's reach for self-awareness. Let's lean into honesty. And let's remember that the most impactful teaching often doesn't come from what we deliver, it comes from who we are.

## A CALL TO ACTION: THIS IS PERSONAL

So, here's your invitation: Embrace "I Before E." Prioritize influence. Redefine effectiveness. And stop clinging to control like it's the only way to keep the room in order. Let go of the illusion that authority alone changes lives, because it doesn't. Influence does.

This book is for the first-year teacher walking into a classroom full of uncertainty. It's for the seasoned educator who's teetering on the edge of burnout, wondering if it still matters. It's for the parent who wants to connect more than correct. It's for the mentor, the coach, the counselor, the community leader, anyone ready to lead with heart, not just with a handbook.

It is not for those looking for quick fixes, magic tricks, or neat little formulas. You won't find those here. Because this work isn't neat. It's not a checklist. It's human. It's messy. It's real.

Your students are watching how you show up. Every day. With every word. With every choice. You might be the most consistent lesson they ever experience. So, choose trust. Choose presence. Choose to be the adult who transforms, not by controlling outcomes, but by cultivating influence.

This isn't about being perfect. It's about being real. Being consistent. Being someone worth listening to.

And here's the final word, the full-circle moment: This is bigger than policy or pedagogy. This is about the way we choose to show up in a world that often forgets what young people truly need. It's not about mastering curriculum guides or compliance checklists. It's about mastering ourselves. Because when we change the way we see young people, we begin to change the way they see themselves.

This is about legacy. About what you leave behind in the hearts and minds of the students you'll never forget, and those who will never forget you.

This is about impact. The kind that doesn't show up on data sheets, but echoes through generations.

This is about humanity. Raw, flawed, beautiful, complicated humanity. Yours. Theirs. Ours.

So let's not just teach young people how to behave.

Let's teach them how to be.

Because in the end, the most powerful lesson you'll ever teach might be the one you didn't plan. It'll be the one they'll never forget.

## THE I BEFORE E FRAMEWORK

*Influence Impacts Effectiveness. Forget About Control.*

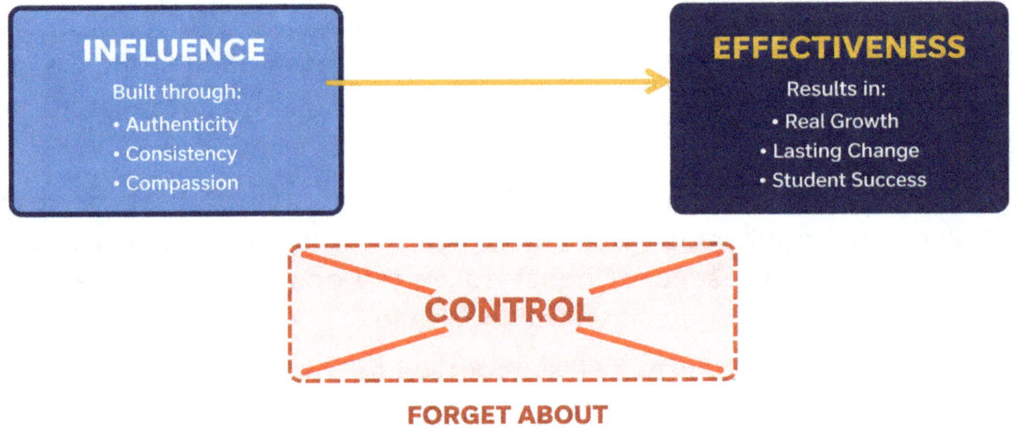

**KEY INSIGHT: When you prioritize INFLUENCE over CONTROL, effectiveness follows naturally through trust, relationship, and genuine growth.**

*THE I BEFORE E FRAMEWORK: INFLUENCE EFFECTIVENESS (FORGET CONTROL)*

CHAPTER 01

# DISCIPLINE | THE ELEPHANT IN THE CLASSROOM

Discipline is the elephant in the classroom, massive, silent, and always present. You can feel it when a student starts testing boundaries before the morning announcements are even over. It's there in the split-second decision of whether to ignore the eyeroll or call it out. It's in the way your heart rate spikes when a confrontation starts to brew, or in the quiet dread of writing yet another referral. Discipline doesn't just loom. It lingers in the corners of our routines, in our tone of voice, and in the rules posted on the wall. It shapes the culture of the room even when no one is misbehaving.

Yet most of us aren't really taught how to deal with it. We're handed policies, not philosophies. We are given strategies, not space to reflect. So, we default to what we know or what feels immediate, even if it doesn't feel right. When discipline arises, it's often in hushed hallway venting or staff meetings filled with frustration. Rarely is it discussed as the complex, deeply human, and foundational part of teaching that it truly is.

But we must name it. We must bring that elephant into the conversation, not as a threat, but as an opportunity. Because the way we approach discipline reveals what we believe about kids: Are they problems to control or people to support? Are we teaching compliance or are we cultivating self-awareness? Facing the discipline question head-on invites us to rethink not just how we respond to misbehavior, but how we build community, create safety, and define respect in our classrooms.

## WHY DISCIPLINE FEELS SO HEAVY

Let's be honest...for many teachers, discipline is the most emotionally draining part of the job. You can spend hours crafting the perfect lesson. You can differentiate it, make it engaging and aligned to the standards. And in a matter of seconds, one behavioral disruption can knock the whole thing off balance. It's like building a delicate house of cards, only to have a gust of wind sweep through the moment the bell rings.

There's a particular kind of weight that comes with discipline. It's not just about handling misbehavior. It's about the pressure of making decisions that can shape a student's path, for better or worse, while the clock ticks and twenty-five other kids are watching. It's the mental load of walking a tightrope between authority and empathy. Teachers are expected to be both the enforcer of rules and the nurturer of growth. It's like carrying a backpack full of bricks, and each brick has a different role: teacher, counselor, mediator, protector, role model, behavior analyst, etc. That weight doesn't get left in the classroom at the end of the day. It follows you home, sits with you at dinner, and echoes in your sleep.

One high school teacher once described it to me like this: It feels like I'm carrying a balance scale in my hands all day. On one side is the need to keep the class focused, safe, and moving forward. On the other hand, is the reality that the student who just disrupted everything might also be the one silently falling apart. Every decision I make tips the scales, and I'm just trying not to let it crash to the floor.

Traditional models of discipline don't lighten that load. If anything, they add more weight. The old-school 'do this or else' mindset demands compliance but rarely earns understanding. It might stop the behavior for a moment, but it often builds resentment, fear, or shame in the long run. And when you see a student get sent out of class day after day, the question shifts from "Why can't they behave?" to "Why aren't we helping them change?"

Picture this: if every time a student made a mistake in math, missed a step in long division or got a fraction wrong, they were immediately removed from class and sent to the principal. We would never stand for it. We would say they need more support, more instruction, more chances. But when it comes to behavior, that logic often disappears. Instead of teaching the skill, we remove the student.

That's the heaviness of discipline. It's not just about behavior, it's about belief. It's about carrying the responsibility to respond in a way that protects the learning environment and honors the humanity of the student in front of you. That's a lot to hold. It's why we need better tools, better systems, and better conversations... not to add more weight, but to help teachers carry it differently.

## THE PURPOSE OF DISCIPLINE ISN'T TO PUNISH

Here's a radical shift that education desperately needs. Discipline is not about control. It's about growth. It's not a power play. It's not about making kids obey. The real purpose of discipline is to guide behavior, to teach students how to navigate conflict, regulate their emotions, and make better choices the next time. Just like we teach math or writing, we must teach the life skills that sit beneath behavior.

Historically, discipline in schools leaned hard into punishment; physical discipline, paddling, standing for hours, even public humiliation. These were all once common practices, rooted in the belief that pain creates order. But over time, we've learned a painful truth: fear might stop a behavior, but it rarely builds character. At best, punishment creates temporary compliance. At worst, it teaches kids that power is something to fear, not something to understand.

Today, the shift is toward a non-physical, reflective form of discipline that invite students to think critically about their actions and the impact those actions have on others.

We don't need to "break" a student's will. We need to build their capacity to manage themselves. A student who throws a chair isn't trying to destroy the classroom. They might be overwhelmed by a frustration they don't know how to name. A student who shuts down and refuses to work might not be lazy. They might be drowning in anxiety. If we respond only to the behavior, we treat the symptom. If we look underneath, we treat the cause.

REAL DISCIPLINE IS ABOUT DIALOGUE, NOT DOMINATION.

## STORY 1: NOT JUST A BAD KID

Mr. McCall, a fifth-grade teacher, had a student named Isaiah who constantly disrupted lessons by talking out of turn, challenging directions, and slamming his desk. The default response had always been to remove him from class. But Mr. McCall started pulling Isaiah aside instead of sending him out. One day, after a particularly loud outburst, Mr. McCall asked, "What's really going on today?" Isaiah shrugged, angry at first, then blurted out, "My mom didn't come home last night again. I was just...mad."

That moment changed everything. Instead of suspension from school, Mr. McCall and Isaiah made a plan together. Isaiah would check in with Mr. McCall every morning. The behavior didn't vanish overnight, but the relationship got stronger. Isaiah started asking for breaks before blowing up. "I'm not just a bad kid," he told Mr. McCall months later. "You actually help me figure stuff out."

## STORY 2: A BROKEN WINDOW AND A BIGGER REPAIR

At a middle school, a student named Laila broke a classroom window in a fit of anger after a heated argument with another student. Normally, Laila would have faced a multi-day suspension and a bill for the damages, but her school practiced restorative discipline.

Laila sat in a circle with her teacher, the class, and a counselor. She had to listen as her classmates talked about how her actions made them feel scared and unsafe. Then she shared why she exploded. It had been the result of a week of bottled-up stress, bullying, and no safe adult to talk to.

She offered an apology, then helped the custodian clean up the damage, and spent the week organizing classroom supplies as a way to give back. "That was harder than getting suspended." She said. "But I think it helped more."

## STORY 3: THE DETOUR THAT SAVED A STUDENT

Coach Daniels, a high school P.E. teacher, noticed one student, Jaylen, repeatedly skipping class or coming in late and agitated. The assistant principal suggested detention. Coach Daniels asked to try something else. He offered Jaylen a deal: if he showed up on time for a week, they'd shoot hoops together after school. Jaylen agreed. By the third day, Jaylen was early to class. By the end of the week, he confided that home had been chaotic, and school was the only place he felt in control, so acting out gave him that feeling. Instead of a discipline file, Jaylen got a mentor. Instead of a punishment, he got a connection. And his behavior started to reflect that shift.

A middle school principal once said it like this: "When I stopped asking, 'How do I get this kid under control?' and started asking, 'What is this kid trying to tell me?'...that's when my entire approach changed." That mindset shift doesn't mean letting students off the hook. It means holding them to high expectations while helping them build the skills to meet them.

## DISCIPLINE AS STRATEGY, NOT SOFTNESS

If a child pushes another student on the playground, we can respond with punishment, a timeout, a loss of recess, a call home. Or, we can treat the moment as a teachable one: Why did you push? What were you feeling? What else could you have done? How can you make things right? That's not being soft. That's being strategic. It turns a bad choice into a better brain. The behavior isn't the full story; it's just the cover. Underneath that angry outburst or quiet defiance is often a child who doesn't yet have the words, the tools, or the trust to handle what they're going through. Discipline done well digs deeper. It doesn't just ask what happened; it asks *why*. Not how do we punish this? But how do we help this student grow from it?

Discipline isn't about overpowering a student; it's about empowering them. Empowering them to recognize their emotions, to own their actions, and to understand how their choices affect others. That's how discipline becomes a tool for transformation, not just correction. Asking the right question can open the door to a stronger student-teacher relationship, and real behavior change. Accountability doesn't require punishment. Real reflection often leads to deeper repair.

The takeaway is that consistency and connection often do more than consequences. That mindset shift doesn't mean lowering expectations. It means keeping the bar high and helping students climb toward it with the tools they need. This is the work. This is the challenge. This is the opportunity to use discipline, not to silence, but to strengthen. Not to punish, but to prepare. Because when we stop trying to control kids, and start teaching them how to control themselves, we're not just managing behavior...we're shaping lives.

## RESTORATIVE, NOT RETRIBUTIVE

Restorative discipline offers a different path; one built not on fear, but on connection. It's grounded in a simple but powerful truth: relationships, not rules, are the foundation of a healthy classroom. Students don't learn best when they're scared of getting in trouble. They learn best when they feel safe, seen, and respected. Traditional discipline asks: What rule was broken and what punishment fits the offense?

**Restorative discipline asks:** Who was affected and how do we repair the harm?

That shift changes everything. It moves the focus from control to community, and from consequences to accountability. It doesn't excuse the behavior. It calls students *into* responsibility, not out of it. It says: "You matter. Your choices matter. And now you have a chance to make it right."

This doesn't mean letting kids off the hook. In fact, restorative approaches often hold students to higher standards; not just for behavior, but for emotional awareness, communication, and follow-through. A student who is asked to reflect, apologize, and take real steps to repair harm learns far more than the one who is simply removed from class and left to stew in isolation.

## A STORY FROM THE HALLWAY: "I DIDN'T KNOW I HURT HER THAT BAD"

At a junior high school, two eighth-grade girls got into a loud, public argument. It ended with one girl crying in the hallway and the other storming off. Normally, both would have been written up and sent home. But their teacher, Ms. Hart, asked for time to handle it restoratively.

The next day, the two girls met privately with Ms. Hart and the school counselor. They each took turns sharing how the argument started, how it escalated, and most importantly, how it felt. One of the girls, Jasmine, had no idea her words had cut so deep. "I didn't know I hurt her that bad," she said, eyes wide. The other girl, Kiara, nodded slowly. "You just kept going, and it felt like I didn't matter at all." Jasmine apologized, and they worked together to come up with a plan not just for repairing the relationship, but for how to handle things differently next time. A week later, they were working together on a group project. They were not best friends, but no longer enemies.

The takeaway from their story is that real accountability begins with real understanding. In a restorative classroom, students learn that their actions have consequences, not just punishments. They learn that their actions affect others. They learn that restoring trust takes effort...and that's a skill worth teaching. This kind of approach takes time. It takes patience. But it builds something stronger than compliance. It builds community. And when students feel they belong, they are far less likely to act out in ways that harm others.

A middle school teacher who started doing short restorative chats after fights put it this way: "The biggest shift came when I stopped seeing behavior as a threat and started seeing it as a signal. That student who blew up during lunch wasn't defiant; he was hurting. When I treated him like someone worth talking to, he started acting like someone who wanted to listen."

The behavior didn't disappear overnight. But it changed because that student felt heard. He felt like someone cared more about his why than just his what. That's what restorative discipline does. It creates space: for repair, for relationship, for growth. And in that space, students learn that they matter, and that others do too.

## DISCIPLINE IS A TEACHABLE MOMENT

Every incident of misbehavior is a chance to teach something. That doesn't mean ignoring boundaries. It means treating misbehavior as part of the learning process. A kid who hasn't learned how to manage frustration isn't all that different from one who hasn't learned how to write a thesis statement, they need modeling, practice, and support. As an analogy, think of GPS, a satellite-based navigation system. When you're driving and take a wrong turn, your GPS doesn't shout, "You blew it! Now you're banned from driving!" Nor does it shut down. Instead, it says, "Recalculating..." It calmly finds another way forward and helps us find a new route. That's exactly what discipline should be. It should help students find a better way to move forward, not punish them for being off track, but guide them back on course. It doesn't ignore the mistake, it adjusts and helps you correct it. Misbehavior doesn't mean a student is "bad." It means something is going on, and it's an opportunity to teach, not just react. Every time a student breaks a rule, interrupts class, or lashes out, we have two choices:

1. Punish them so they fear doing it again.
2. Teach them so they understand what went wrong and how to do better next time. The second option takes more work, but it builds better people, not just better students.

## WHAT MISBEHAVIOR REALLY MEANS

Think of behavior like any other skill. Just like kids don't come to school knowing how to do algebra or write essays, they don't automatically know how to:

- Handle anger
- Share attention
- Apologize
- Sit still when they're overwhelmed
- Walk away instead of yelling

They have to learn those things, and learning takes practice, support, and mistakes. The same could be said for some adults.

## REAL-WORLD, HUMAN-SIZED TECHNIQUES

Here are some simple ways teachers can treat misbehavior as a teachable moment instead of just a problem to fix:

### 1. The "Pause and Ask" Method

Instead of reacting in frustration, take a breath and ask:

- "What's going on right now?"
- "What were you trying to do?"
- "What is a better way you could have handled that?"

**Why it works:** It gives the student space to reflect. It turns correction into a conversation.

### 2. Model What You Want to See

If a student yells, you shouldn't yell back. Show calm. Show control. Show what self-regulation looks like.

**Why it works:** Kids learn from what we do, not just what we say.

### 3. Redirect, Don't Just Remove

Instead of just sending a student out of class, try giving a quiet moment away to reset, and then bring them back with a clear plan:

- "Take five to cool off. When you come back, let's figure out how to keep this day going strong."

**Why it works:** It teaches that a mistake doesn't mean exile; it means repair and return.

**4. Use "Do" Instead of "Don't."**

Instead of just saying, "Don't talk when I'm talking," try:

- "Let's all practice listening first so everyone can be heard."

**Why it works:** It gives students something to aim for, not just something to avoid.

## ONE QUICK STORY: FROM BLOW-UP TO BUY-IN

A ninth grader named Malik had a habit of throwing his notebook when he got frustrated with work. One day, instead of writing him up, his teacher pulled him aside and said, "You don't have to throw your notebook to show you're stuck. Just say, 'I need help.' Can we try that next time?"

Malik nodded. The next week, he raised his hand and quietly said, "I'm stuck." That small moment was a win. That is what a teachable moment looks like. Every student is going to get off track sometimes. Our job isn't to "fix" them; it's to help them learn how to get back on track. When discipline becomes part of learning, not just punishment, students don't just behave better... they grow better.

## DISCIPLINE IS EQUITY WORK

It's no secret that punitive discipline practices have disproportionately affected students of color, students with disabilities, and students from marginalized communities. If we keep using the same outdated approaches, we'll keep getting the same inequitable outcomes. Shifting to restorative and relational approaches is not just pedagogical; it's moral. It's about building schools where all students feel respected, supported, and capable of success. Walk into almost any school office on any given day, and you'll notice a pattern, though not everyone will name it out loud. Too often, the same kinds of students are sent out of class, written up, suspended, or labeled "disruptive." Black and Brown students. Boys. Students with IEPs. English language learners. Kids navigating poverty.

The faces of discipline reflect deeper truths about the systems we live in. This is not a coincidence, it's a pattern. It's not about a few "bad apples." It's about a tree rooted in inequity. We can't talk about discipline without talking about race, power, and bias. We can't claim to care about kids if we're ignoring the data and the stories behind it.

## THE REALITY: DISPARITY ISN'T RANDOM

Across the country, data consistently shows that:

Black students are more likely to be suspended for the same behaviors as their White peers. Google any statistic for any urban city. Students of color are more often punished for subjective infractions, things like "defiance" or "attitude." While white students are more often redirected. Students with disabilities are disproportionately disciplined, especially in schools that rely heavily on exclusionary practices. These aren't isolated cases. These are national patterns, and they send a clear message to kids, "Some of you are too much, too loud, too angry, too broken."

## WHAT THAT FEELS LIKE IN A CLASSROOM

Imagine being a Black girl who gets told to "watch her tone" for asking a question. Imagine being a Latino student who hears classmates joke about "getting deported," and when he gets upset and raises his voice, he's the one sent out of the classroom. Imagine being a student with ADHD who's trying to stay focused, but the second he blurts something out, the teacher sighs and sends him to the hallway... again. Over time, these moments build up. They teach students that school is a place where their behavior is policed, but their voices aren't heard. Where their presence is managed, but not valued.

## WHAT REAL EQUITY LOOKS LIKE

Equity in discipline means asking harder questions: Why are we responding to this student's behavior with punishment when that student's behavior requires patience?

Whose "normal" are we centering in this classroom? Are we making space for different ways of expressing emotion, asking questions, or being heard? Shifting to restorative and relational approaches is more than just a "best practice." It's a moral imperative. It's saying we will not keep treating behavior like a crime and certain students like suspects.

## HUMAN-CENTERED SHIFTS THAT SUPPORT EQUITY

Here are some grounded ways to build more equitable discipline practices:

### 1. Slow Down the Snap Judgment

When a student misbehaves, take a moment before reacting. Ask yourself:

- Would I respond the same way if this student looked or spoke differently?
- Am I seeing disrespect, or am I reacting to discomfort?

**Why it matters:** Bias often shows up in split-second decisions. Slowing down helps you choose connection over reaction.

### 2. Rebuild the Definition of "Respect"

Not all cultures express respect in the same way. Not every student makes eye contact. Not every voice is soft. Volume and tone can land differently. Questions don't always equal defiance. Respect is subjective, not one-size-fits-all.

**Why it matters:** Equity starts by validating that students can be different and still be respectful.

### 3. Make Relationships the Rule

Instead of asking, "How do I get this student to comply?" ask:

- "What's our relationship like?"
- "Does this student trust me enough to listen?"

**Why it matters:** Students are more likely to change when they feel connected. Relationships don't just soften behavior; they shape it.

## A REAL MOMENT THAT CHANGED A SCHOOL

At a high school in Oakland, California, a principal reviewed suspension data and saw a hard truth: nearly 90% of suspensions were Black male students. Same rules, same school, wildly different outcomes. Instead of blaming the students, the school brought in restorative practices. Teachers were trained to lead listening circles, not just for conflict, but for connection. The school began checking in with students before behavior problems started. They asked students what respect looked like to them. By the next year, suspensions dropped by 60%. More importantly, Black students said they finally felt like they belonged. This Is the work.

Discipline isn't just about misbehavior... it's about power. Equity work means recognizing when that power has been unevenly used and choosing to do better. If we want schools where all students feel safe, supported, and seen, we must make discipline not just about fixing problems, but about changing patterns. When students walk into classrooms where they're not punished, but understood, they don't just behave better. They believe more in themselves.

**Let's tell the truth:** teaching is hard. It's early mornings, late nights, and thousands of decisions in between. It's managing moods, grading work, and navigating pressure from every direction. It's balancing the needs of thirty students while keeping your own head above water. It's emotional, unpredictable, and at times, deeply exhausting. But it's also worth it, because few professions carry the power to shape futures like this one. Discipline isn't just about misbehavior. It's about power; who holds it, how it's used, and who it affects. Every time we respond to a student's behavior, we're making choices not just about consequences, but about values.

Are we choosing control or connection?

Are we choosing silence or conversation?

Are we reinforcing old patterns or creating new possibilities?

Equity work in schools means stepping back and asking, Where has discipline gone wrong? Who is it failing? And then having the courage to do something different, even if it's harder, slower, or more uncomfortable. Because the truth is: problems don't get fixed by punishment. They get fixed through understanding. Change Happens Through Understanding.

When students feel understood, they're more likely to:

- Trust their teachers
- Open up about their challenges
- Take responsibility for their actions
- Believe they belong, even when they mess up

It's easy to correct a student. It's much harder and more meaningful to understand them. Understanding doesn't mean excusing harm or lowering expectations. It means asking better questions:

- What's behind this behavior?
- What support does this student need?
- How can I respond in a way that builds them up, rather than shutting them down?

This is the difference between reaction and relationship.

## CHANGING PATTERNS, NOT JUST MOMENTS

Too often, schools focus on fixing the moment by quieting the class, stopping the disruption, and getting through the day. But the more important goal is to change the pattern.

That starts with:

- Seeing discipline as part of learning, not separate from it

- Recognizing that power must be paired with compassion
- Understanding that every student who walks into your classroom brings a story, and that story shapes how they show up

## A MINDSET THAT MOVES MOUNTAINS

When a student acts out, and you choose curiosity instead of anger, that's the work. When you pull a student aside instead of sending them out, that's the work. When you hold firm boundaries but speak with dignity, that's the work. When a student who once shut down now opens up, even just a little, that is the result of the work. Teaching isn't just delivering lessons. It's delivering hope… one student, one choice, one relationship at a time.

## THE POWER YOU HOLD

You don't have to solve everything. But every time you respond with understanding instead of the assumption, you're reshaping the classroom into a place where students feel safe, seen, and capable of growth.

When kids know they're more than their worst moment, they begin to act like it. They begin to rise. And in classrooms where students aren't just punished but understood, they don't just behave better. They believe more in themselves. The Discipline We Model Matters. Teachers model discipline every day, not just in how we respond to students, but in how we carry ourselves. Are we calm when things go sideways? Do we model apology and repair when we mess up? Do we show students what it looks like to disagree respectfully, to stay grounded in conflict, to lead with empathy? Discipline is not about getting students to sit down and be quiet. It's about helping them stand up (and on business, when needed) and be responsible. And, if we do it right, the "elephant" becomes a shared conversation, not a looming threat.

In every classroom, long before a student acts out, long before a rule is broken, there's already a lesson unfolding. It's not written on the board. It's not part of the curriculum. But it's the one kids are watching the most closely: how the adults handle themselves. As teachers, we model discipline every single day, not just in how we respond to students, but in how we carry ourselves.

When a lesson falls apart, do we stay composed or spiral with it?

When a student pushes back, do we listen or power through?

When we get something wrong, do we apologize, or pretend it didn't happen?

Every moment is a mirror. Students are constantly learning from how we handle stress, how we manage conflict, and how we treat people when it's hard to do so. They're not just learning from our lessons; they're learning from our leadership.

## ADULTS LEAD FIRST

If we want students to learn self-regulation, we have to show them what it looks like.

Want them to stay calm? Stay calm yourself.

Want them to take accountability? Own your mistakes when you make them.

Want them to repair harm? Model that. Say, "I was short with you earlier. That wasn't fair. Let's try again."

These small moments teach volumes. They show students that discipline is not about control, it's about growth, and it starts with us. If we model 'crashing out' on or in front of students, we cannot be shocked when we see or experience the same energy.

## THE ELEPHANT WE CAN'T IGNORE

At the start of this chapter, we named it, "Discipline, The Elephant in the Classroom." It's always there, quietly shaping the tone, the trust, the entire learning environment. Too often, that elephant feels like a threat:

- Who's going to act up next?
- How much time will I lose handling it?
- What will people think of me if I "lose control" of the room?

But it doesn't have to be that way. If we shift from reaction to reflection, from punishment to purpose, from control to connection, then the elephant doesn't loom. It leads. It becomes a shared conversation about what it means to be a part of a learning community. It becomes something students participate in, not something they fear.

## FINAL THOUGHT: DISCIPLINE THROUGH UNDERSTANDING

Discipline done right isn't about silence; it's about strength. Not about compliance, but character. Not about controlling kids but teaching them how to lead themselves. And that starts with us. If we want classrooms where students make better choices, we must be adults who show them what better choices look like. If we want classrooms rooted in mutual respect, we must be the ones to plant that seed. If we want change, we must be willing to model it.

Because in the end, the discipline we model is the discipline they carry. And when we center understanding, not fear, we don't just manage behavior, we change lives.

CHAPTER 02

# ORDER AND LAW (REIMAGINED) FROM COURTROOMS TO CLASSROOMS

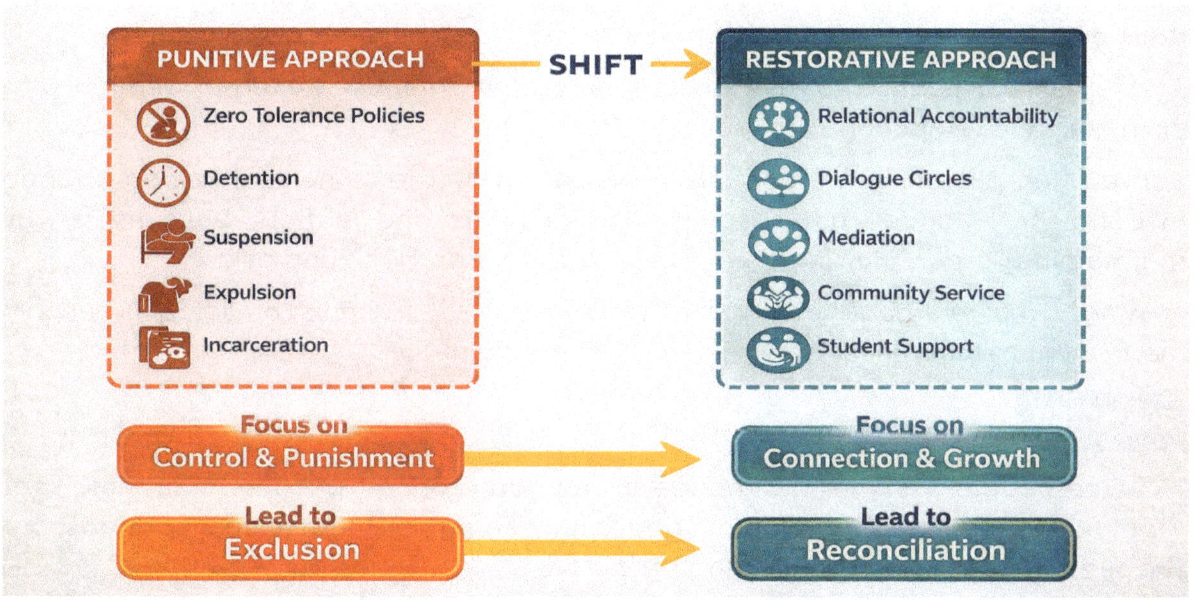


*FROM PUNISHMENT TO RESTORATION:*
*CHANGING THE SYSTEM, CHANGING THE OUTCOME.*

When I led professional development for school leaders, I often started with a simple, almost playful question:

"What's the longest-running scripted American primetime TV show?"

Most people don't get it right. The real answer? *The Simpsons*, still going after more than three decades. Right behind it, in the world of live-action, are *Law & Order: SVU* and the original *Law & Order.* Those shows have lasted for a reason and it's not by accident. They reflect a mindset baked into American culture.

We've grown up watching courtroom drama unfold on screens big and small. We live in a culture that's been taught to believe in "law and order" as the standard for how things should run. Someone breaks the rules. A judge listens. A sentence is handed down, " two years," "five years," "life." Justice is delivered swiftly, cleanly, and with the bang of a gavel.

Without realizing it, that model has shaped the way we think discipline should work, even in our schools. But what happens when we bring that same thinking into our schools? It sounds something like this: "You were disrespectful? That's two days out." "Late again? You've got detention."

In other words: *You did the crime. Now, do the time.* But we're not dealing with criminals. We're dealing with kids.

I've often played into that system myself, with little to no real lasting change in behavior. I handed out suspensions like flyers and leaflets, believing I was maintaining "order." But at some point, I had to step back and ask:

*What's my real goal here? Am I trying to control students, or actually support them? Am I helping them grow, or just pushing them out?*

## THE SHIFT

Some people assume the change in me came once I became a parent. That moment was powerful, holding my daughter, seeing her innocence, her needs, but the seeds were planted earlier than that.

I remember one moment vividly. It was 2005. I was sitting in training at a residential school when the facilitator asked, "Is the work we do personal or professional?"

Without hesitation, nearly everyone in the room said, "Professional." I agreed. It made sense. We were trained to stay objective, avoid getting "too close," and to keep boundaries. That was the norm. But then the facilitator hit us with something I'll never forget.

He said, "*You work with kids every day. You see their trauma, their home life, their fears. You, your reactions, and decisions are also impacted by your experiences, your trauma, your home life, and your fears.* You have custody of them for most of the day. How is that not personal?"

That line hit hard. That question rewired something in me. I had to re-examine myself, my experiences, my reactions, my decisions, and how they were impacted by my own upbringing, home life, traumas, triggers, and fears.

*How could I say I care about kids, and then turn around and treat them like a problem to remove? Like a number on a referral sheet?*

We always talk about "three chances." But what happens after the third? When my daughter doesn't listen after three reminders, do I pack up her pull-ups and onesies and send her out on her way? Absolutely not.

I might take a breath. I might need a break. But I keep trying. I stay with her. Because she's mine.

And that made me ask: *Why don't we treat students with the same kind of patience and persistence we show our own children?*

## A TURNING POINT

Another shift came from a conversation with a colleague. We were talking about school discipline, and I said something like, "We still have to hold students accountable."

They shot back: "But how can you hold a child accountable for something they've never been taught in the first place?"

That one sat with me. They weren't saying ignore behavior. They were saying: *Make sure you're still teaching.*

That's when I realized our approach wasn't working. Especially in my role at that time as the Dean of Students, I saw how often discipline was more about punishment than growth. That was also the perspective of those I worked side by side, with teachers who saw me as security, as the enforcer. I was the muscle, the proverbial thumb-breaker to swoop in and handle business. We weren't helping kids understand their choices. We were simply reacting. Part of my realization: There must be some teaching, some instruction to properly manage expectations, to be fair and equitable.

So, I wrote a new vision for our school's approach:

> *"We believe discipline isn't just about consequences. It's about learning. We believe it's not just about following rules, but about understanding why good decisions matter. We believe discipline should include, not exclude. We believe our job is to guide students toward reflection and growth. We believe in healing, not just correcting. We believe in planting seeds, even in difficult soil."*

That became the new foundation.

## DISCIPLINE ISN'T A JAIL SENTENCE. IT'S A SECOND CHANCE.

If you looked up the definition of discipline, one of the definitions would be "a branch of knowledge, typically one studied in higher education. Another would be "the practice of training." Here's the truth: traditional school discipline mirrors the justice system way too closely; and for marginalized students, that resemblance isn't just symbolic, it's real, and it's harmful. In too many schools, discipline doesn't feel like guidance, it feels like prosecution. Picture it: a student makes a mistake, and instead of being pulled into a conversation, they're pulled into an office. No questions. No context. Just a cold decision handed down like a sentence. It's as if the classroom turned into a courtroom overnight, with the principal, or whoever has the decision-making authority, playing judge, jury, and enforcer.

There's no space for understanding, no room for repair... just punishment. A missed homework assignment becomes defiance. Talking back is disorderly conduct. A hoodie, a side-eye, a slick comment, a curse word, a sigh... and suddenly that student is labeled a problem. Sometimes the smallest misstep gets escalated like a criminal act. When that happens, it's not about learning; it's about control. And that control falls hardest on students of color, who are too often seen as threats before they're seen as children. What should be a place for growth becomes a place for judgment, and in that kind of system, kids don't get second chances. They get records and a "sheet."

If you've never heard of the school-to-prison pipeline, understand this: it's not just a buzzword. It's a system that pushes kids, especially kids of color, out of classrooms and into jail cells. Here's how it works: A student talks back, gets suspended. Another wears a hoodie, gets labeled a "threat." One more skips class, gets suspended or even expelled. These are minor things, but they lead to major consequences. Missing school leads to missing more school. Missing more school results in lost instructional time, disengagement, failing grades, retention, and more. It all leads to a higher likelihood of dropping out. Which then students at a much higher risk of poor choices, including being around, influenced by, and/or engaging in unlawful activity.

This pipeline is not about behavior. It's about bias. Black students are nearly four times more likely than White students to be suspended, even for the same actions. Latino students face similar gaps. And once a kid is suspended or expelled, they're more likely to fall behind, get policed more heavily, and eventually end up in the justice system. It's like a conveyor belt moving kids out of school and into prison... and it starts shockingly early, sometimes in elementary school.

Think of it this way: if schools are supposed to be safe havens, then this system is flipping the script. It's turning schools into entry points for incarceration. That's not safety... that's a trap. Some would argue that it is doing what it is designed to do, not close the education gap, but perpetuate it.

**And here's the thing:** Kids don't grow when they're pushed out. They grow when they're pulled in.

We've got to stop thinking like judges and start thinking like healers. When a student "acts out," it's not usually because they want to cause problems. It's because something underneath is bubbling up.

A doctor doesn't kick a patient out of the ER because they're bleeding. They stop the bleeding, ask questions, and dig deeper to understand the root of the issue. We need to do the same. Anyone with children who have experienced a newborn will tell you, even though babies cannot talk, there are variations in their crying that communicate everything you need to know if you are aware and listening. There is a cry for hunger, for food, for sleep, for pain, to be changed, etc. They all sound different. However, they may all sound the same to a rookie or untrained ear.

Behavior is communication, and too often, we punish the symptom without treating the cause.

We need to stop being so quick to throw kids out and start asking what they're going through. We need to replace judgment with curiosity. Replace isolation with support. Replace punishment with purpose.

## TO EDUCATORS: THIS WORK IS PERSONAL

We have to ask ourselves, with honesty and courage: *Are we building schools that feel like communities, or courtrooms? Are our classrooms places of healing or holding cells? When a student messes up, do they feel safe to grow or scared to return?*

Because let's be real, handing out detentions and suspensions like sentencing slips isn't teaching. That's not discipline. That's damage. And our students, especially our Black and Brown students, have been carrying that weight for far too long.

Discipline should never be about order & law. It should never be about control for control's sake. It should be about care, about correction with dignity, about reminding students they belong, even when they're struggling.

It's time to shift.

From control to connection. From punishment to purpose. From law and order to love and understanding.

Let's stop treating kids like problems to be fixed, and start seeing them as people to be guided. Let's be the adults who don't just correct, but commit. Let's be the adults who show up, who stay, who choose compassion, even when it's hard. Especially when it's hard.

Because the real work of education isn't about power; it's about partnership. And discipline, when done right, doesn't push students out. It brings them back in. It says *You still matter. You still belong. Let's keep going.*

That's the kind of teaching that changes lives. That's the kind of teaching our kids deserve. And that's the kind of teaching we must choose every single day.

CHAPTER 03

# GOOD COP/BAD COP | FIRM BUT FAIR

We've all heard the phrase "good cop/bad cop." In its original use, it describes two people working together, one acts tough, the other acts kind, to push someone toward a decision. It's a setup, a performance. One lays down the pressure, the other offers relief. Together, they control the situation.

Now, let's bring that into the classroom. Except here's the catch: we don't have a partner to play the other role. We're the only adults in the room, and we have to wear both hats, firm and fair, at the same time. The good cop and the bad cop live in the same person, YOU.

But here's the real lesson: teaching isn't about playing roles. It's not about being fake or switching masks. It's about finding a steady balance that builds respect without fear, and structure without shame. That's what the good cop/bad cop idea misses when applied to education... it assumes manipulation. But real teaching is built on relationship, not strategy.

This isn't about being two different people. It's about being one consistent person who knows when to draw the line and when to offer a hand.

Because here's the truth: if you're too soft, students will test you. And once they know you'll fold, they'll treat every rule like a suggestion. On the flip side, if you come down too hard, if every mistake is a punishment, they'll stop trying altogether. They'll check out. Either way, you lose the opportunity to lead them.

Real growth for our students lives in the middle where expectations are clear, consequences are meaningful, and compassion is constant. That's where we do our best work.

## BALANCING THE TWO: FIRM BUT FAIR

This technique has a few versions, such as warm & demanding and warm/strict. Being "firm but fair" isn't about swinging between extremes. It's about holding consistent expectations with compassion. Your firmness communicates structure and stability. Your fairness communicates respect and humanity. Students need both.

I've seen it firsthand. When I was a student, I could spot a pushover teacher from down the hallway. We didn't call them that out loud, but we knew. We tested limits. And when we found one? We shared that info with others, like breaking news. "Oh, you got Mr. Jenkins? Man, just tell him you forgot your homework... he'll let you slide." That kind of teacher loses control fast.

But on the flip side, there were the "Stone Cold Steve Austin" types, the ones who ran their classrooms like a boot camp. No room for questions. No grace. Every mistake was met with punishment. And sure, we didn't test them, but we didn't trust them either. You can't learn from someone you're scared of.

Somewhere between those two is where we need to live.

## WHY A COP? WHY NOT A HEALER?

Let's take a moment to challenge the metaphor itself. Why are we comparing our role to a cop in the first place?

Now, I get it..."good cop/bad cop" is a common phrase, one that is easy to recognize. But if we're being honest, the image of a cop, especially in classrooms with Black and Brown children, carries a weight we can't ignore. Authority. Control. Surveillance. Compliance by force. That might work in an interrogation room, but it doesn't build trust in a classroom.

So let me offer a better metaphor: not a cop, but a healer.

Think like a nurse. Like a doctor. Think about what happens when a child falls and scrapes their knee on the playground. We don't yell. We don't lecture. We don't give out detention slips for tripping. We assess the injury. We clean the wound. We give care. And maybe... we teach the child how to run more carefully next time.

**The goal isn't punishment; it's healing and growth.**

That same principle should guide our response when a student acts out. Their behavior is usually a symptom, not the whole story. Maybe they're frustrated because they don't understand the material. Maybe they're coming off a rough night at home. Maybe they're angry because they don't have the language yet to express their feelings.

There was a student, let's call him Marcus. He was bright, witty, and full of personality. But he also had a sharp edge to him. Anytime a teacher tried to redirect him, he snapped back, quick with sarcasm and always ready to challenge authority. Over time, his name became familiar in staff meetings, mostly for the wrong reasons. Teachers labeled him as disrespectful. Some stopped trying. He was written off and sent out of class more than he was taught in it.

But one teacher who had seen this pattern before chose a different route. Instead of another referral, they asked Marcus to stay after class. No lecture. No raised voice. Just a quiet conversation. The teacher asked, "What's going on with you?"

At first, Marcus shrugged it off, guarded like most kids who are in survival mode. But slowly, the truth came out. His mother had been hospitalized, and he was bouncing between relatives. His home life was unpredictable. He was scared and angry, and school had become the only place where he could exert control... by pushing back.

That conversation didn't erase the challenges overnight. But it changed the teacher's lens. Instead of reacting to Marcus's behavior with frustration, the teacher responded to Marcus with structure and support. Boundaries stayed in place, but they were delivered with calm, not anger; with care, not punishment. And over time, Marcus started to shift. Not because he was forced to, but because he finally felt seen.

Now contrast that with another student; let's call her Tiana.

Tiana was different from Marcus. She was charming, clever, and fully aware of how to work a room, especially when it came to pushing boundaries. She wasn't struggling emotionally the same way Marcus was. In fact, Tiana had a solid support system at home and plenty of academic ability. But she liked to test limits. She'd joke during lessons, disrupt transitions, and playfully challenge the rules, not out of trauma, but because she wanted control without responsibility.

With Tiana, the same teacher used a different approach. There was still respect and still patience, but there was also a firm line drawn early. Expectations were crystal clear. The consequences weren't loud or harsh, but they were consistent. When Tiana acted out, she lost privileges. When she followed through, she earned trust. And when she pushed back, the teacher didn't fold.

It didn't take long for Tiana to adjust. She realized that this wasn't a power game. She couldn't charm or argue her way out of every situation. And once she saw that, her energy shifted. She began to lead in positive ways. She was still bold and still vibrant, but she had more direction and purpose.

That's the balance. Marcus needed compassion first, then structure. Tiana needed structure first, then space to grow. Both students were respected. Both were held accountable. But the teacher didn't use a one-size-fits-all response. They read the room. They read the child.

*CHECK FOR WOUNDS, NOT JUST RULES. ASK WHAT HAPPENED, NOT JUST WHAT WAS BROKEN.*

This is the essence of being firm and fair. It's not about being soft. It's not about being strict. It's about being intentional, responsive. and human. While every student needs something slightly different, they all need to know one thing for sure. They need to know that: You see them. You believe in them. You're not afraid to lead them.

The natural consequence of a scraped knee is pain. The natural consequence of disrupting class might be missing out on the knowledge and understanding that comes from direct instruction, a fun activity, or both. But if we don't help students connect their actions to outcomes, and give them a path to do better next time, then all they walk away with is shame. And shame doesn't lead to reflection. It leads to retreat.

Your classroom should be a place where students feel safe enough to stumble and supported enough to get back up.

So maybe the real question isn't, "Am I the good cop or the bad cop?"

Maybe the question is: "Am I responding to this child's behavior in a way that heals or harms?"

Choose healing. That's where the power is.

## DON'T BE A PUSHOVER; BUT DON'T BE A BULLY

Yes, give students a chance to fix their actions. But do not hand out passes like candy. Some kids don't know the difference between grace and a green light. You've got to help them learn that difference, and that lesson starts with you.

Teachers should hold students accountable because they care, not despite it. That distinction matters. Accountability rooted in care sends a very different message than punishment rooted in frustration. And students can feel the difference, even if they don't always know how to name it.

One teacher put it plainly to their class: "I'm not letting you get away with everything because I see more in you than that. You're capable of better, and it's my job to help you get there."

That kind of message, spoken with firmness and without judgment, sticks with students. It tells them: "I see your potential, not just your problems." It draws a line without cutting the connection. It reminds students that boundaries aren't barriers; they are investments. And when those boundaries come with consistency and care, they build trust instead of fear.

That's what accountability looks like in a classroom that's rooted in relationship. Not just calling students out, but calling them up.

At the same time, don't go chasing respect by being mean. You don't earn respect by belittling students. That's how you lose them. One at first, then two, and before you know it, you're teaching a room full of silent resentment.

## TEACH, DON'T PUNISH

Every decision made in a classroom should be guided by a core question: "Am I teaching this student, or am I punishing them?"

It's a simple question, but one that can change everything.

Punishment may stop a behavior temporarily, but it rarely creates long-term growth. Teaching, on the other hand, transforms behavior. It offers understanding, correction, and tools to do better next time. The goal isn't obedience, it's development.

There was a student, let's call him Jalen, who constantly interrupted class discussions. Not with malice, but with excitement. He always had a thought, an opinion, a question; he just couldn't seem to wait his turn. Some teachers saw it as defiance. Others assumed he was trying to steal attention. He was written up multiple times for "disruption."

But one teacher saw something different. Instead of defaulting to punishment, they sat Jalen down and listened. Together, they came up with a solution: a notepad on his desk where he could jot down his ideas during discussions and share them at specific points in the lesson. Within weeks, the interruptions faded, and Jalen remained engaged without being silenced, learning time and place.

That's not lowering expectations. That's teaching a student how to meet them.

That's the difference between control and connection. Between compliance and growth. The classroom should never be a space where students are afraid to mess up. It should be a space where they learn how to adjust when they do.

A consequence without context teaches fear. A response rooted in clarity and care teaches accountability.

## KNOW YOUR BOUNDARIES. OWN YOUR ROLE.

Structure matters. Boundaries matter. And the students who need them most are often the ones who push hardest against them. That's why educators must lead with both consistency and compassion.

When teachers are clear about their expectations, consistent in their responses, and grounded in their own values, students learn to trust the classroom environment. Not because it's perfect, but because it's predictable and safe. That trust opens the door to deeper relationships and real learning.

This doesn't mean educators need to fit into a rigid role. You can hold high standards and extend grace. You can challenge your students and still let them know you care. You can correct them without shaming them.

One teacher, faced with a student who had skipped multiple assignments and ignored feedback, didn't start with penalties. Instead, the teacher said, "You're too smart and too important to let this slide. So, we're going to figure this out, together." That student, who had grown used to either being punished or ignored, finally leaned in.

Students don't always need traditional consequences. Sometimes, they need to be called back to themselves. That's what true guidance looks like.

So, educators must ask themselves:

- Are you showing up as the good cop, offering comfort and avoiding conflict?
- Are you acting as the bad cop, only enforcing rules without building relationships?
- Or maybe, just maybe, it's time to stop seeing yourself as a cop at all.

Maybe it's time to show up as a guide, a coach, a healer, someone who holds students accountable not to punish them, but to prepare them. Someone who sees the child behind the behavior, the potential behind the misstep.

That's where the real work lives.

Every educator must check their own approach. What do your actions communicate? Are you building compliance or character? Are you shaping behavior, or just reacting to it?

When you find the balance that reflects your values and affirms your students' humanity, don't let it go. Stand in it. Lead from it. Build with it.

Because once you get this right...once you embrace being firm and fair, with purpose and heart, you won't just be managing a classroom.

You'll be changing lives.

CHAPTER 04

# POLICING VS. MEDICAL APPROACH

Now let's push this analogy a step further.

Picture this: A student walks into class with their energy off. They slam their backpack down, snap at a classmate, roll their eyes at you, and refuse to do any work.

Now, pause. *What's your next move?*

Do you write them up? Kick them out? Or do you pull them aside and ask, "What's really going on?" Decisions, decisions! Everyone is looking.

Right there, you're standing at a fork in the road: Are you stepping in as the doctor... or as the cop?

This might seem like a strange comparison, but hang with me for a moment. This is not about bashing police or making doctors out to be heroes. Nor is this an attempt to brush all officers with a broad stroke. Some officers inherently possess counselor-like, soft people skills, with high levels of discernment. It's not about the job titles; it's about the mindset and approach.

Cops are trained to gain control. To keep order. This is not inclusive of specialized-trained school resource officers. Traditional officers are typically called when something's already gone wrong. Their first job isn't to heal, it's to assess if laws have been broken and respond based on the rules of law and consequences.

Doctors, though? They tend to approach situations differently. They're trained to diagnose. They don't walk into a room asking, "What rule did you break?" They ask, "What hurts?" They look at the symptoms. They ask questions. They look deeper before they decide how to help.

Now think about school discipline. Think about how we react when students misbehave.

Do we step in ready to issue a consequence, like a cop? Or do we slow down, listen, and look for the root cause, like a doctor?

## TWO DIFFERENT OUTCOMES, ONE BIG DIFFERENCE

Let's talk about how mindset changes everything.

Take a student who is always late. In a policing mindset, that could be read as defiance. Responses like, "You know the rule. You broke it. Now take this detention and learn your lesson," imply a very matter-of-fact, black-and-white response. It's quick, it's cold, and it doesn't ask a single question. We ignore the initial direct consequence that may have been present: missed work and class time. The student has missed part of the lesson. The student has missed instructional time that cannot be replaced.

But let's look at that same student through a different lens, a medical mindset, a human mindset. We stop and ask, *What is the root cause here? Why is this student showing up late every day?* Not with sarcasm, but with sincerity. Because maybe, and most often, that lateness has a story.

Maybe they are up before sunrise, getting their little brother and sister dressed, making sure they eat before catching their own bus. Maybe mom works the night shift, and they're holding down the household until she gets home. Maybe they get bullied and come later to avoid the rush of the crowd. Maybe the city bus is late again because that's the only reliable transportation option. Or maybe they're just tired, physically, emotionally, and spiritually... because life outside school isn't soft or simple.

Same behavior. *Two different responses. One says, You failed. The other says, You're carrying a lot; how can I help? What support do you need?* One can feel like the door is slammed in a kid's face. While the other can open the door and pull out a chair. When we lead with judgment, we miss the story, often because we are not interested in the story. But when we lead with curiosity, when we ask questions, we discover resilience, strength, and even brilliance buried under the weight of survival.

We've got to remember not every behavior is a choice. Sometimes it's a response and/or trauma response. Sometimes it's a symptom. Sometimes it's a cry for help that doesn't know how to be expressed in "school-appropriate" language. And when we treat every struggle like a violation or an infraction, we turn our backs on the very students who need us most.

The difference isn't just in how we react; it's in what kind of adults we decide to be.

Are we showing up like wardens? Or are we showing up like allies?

Because for our students, especially our children of color, that difference can and will mean everything.

## WHY THIS MATTERS, ESPECIALLY FOR OUR STUDENTS

Let's keep it a buck. (aka keep it 100, aka let's be honest). When students are treated like suspects, not learners, not young Kings and Queens, they are being conditioned, and they know it. They can feel it in their core. It's in the way adults talk to them, the way they're watched, and the way they're disciplined. The message lands loud and clear: *We don't trust you.*

*Who gets that message the most?* Marginalized students. Often, students with IEPs (Individualized Education Programs). The children who are carrying the weight of trauma that didn't start in the classroom, but shows up there; It shows up during lunch and recess. These are the children most likely to get hit with the "policing approach," the heavier tone, the 'label' shared amongst teachers and staff, the immediate threat of suspension. They are seen as problems to manage, not people to understand. And once that label sticks, it follows them everywhere. I worked with someone who abused his title, power, and privilege to inadvertently cause harm. We will call him Dean Disrespectful. Dean Disrespectful used a label in reference to a group of 14-year-old girls who were friends and who had been in multiple incidents together and separately. He so eloquently named the girls, this group of freshmen girls, the terrible 10. When mentioned, everyone knew who he was referring to, and most folks began to refer to them as such.

That's not equity. That's not care. That's harm... plain and simple.

Imagine if a hospital treated patients like that. Imagine walking into the Emergency Room with a broken arm, and instead of getting help, you're told to leave because your injury is "disruptive," and you are making a mess. That would be outrageous. But that's exactly how too many students are treated when their struggles show up through their behavior. Instead of asking *what happened to you*? Adults jump to *what's wrong with you*?

You can't claim to be about student growth while relying on punishment as your go-to move. Growth takes patience. It takes presence. It takes people willing to sit with the hard stuff and say, "You're still welcome here. Let's figure this out."

Kicking a student out doesn't fix what's wrong; it just hides it. And often, it makes things worse. If school isn't the safest place for a child to struggle, where is?

## THE CHOICE WE MAKE

Every time a student acts out, raises their voice, shuts down, or walks out, we are being asked a quiet question: *Will you punish me... or will you try to understand me?*

Most kids won't say it out loud. They won't have the words, but their behavior is speaking volumes for them, whatever action we take next... that response carries weight. It tells them who they are. It tells them who we are. It tells them who we see when we look at them. It tells them whether school is a place that sees, values, and nurtures them or endures and tolerates them.

We like to talk about discipline as if it's neutral. Like it's just a policy. But it's not. It's a mirror. It reflects our beliefs about children, about race, about class, about control, about care; and that mirror can either show kids a version of themselves that is worthy of patience and growth, or one that's always in trouble, always "too much," always getting it wrong.

Discipline should never be about asserting power. It should be about extending guidance. Not about making students smaller, but helping them grow stronger. Not about removing them from the room, but restoring their place within it.

Think about it like this: When someone shows signs of pain, a doctor doesn't scold them for limping. They ask, "Where does it hurt?" They investigate. They treat. They follow up. That's care. That's what healing looks like.

So why should it be any different in our classrooms?

Let's stop acting like every outburst is just misbehavior and start recognizing it as communication. Let's choose the doctor's mindset: curiosity over judgment, support over shame, healing over harm.

Because our kids, especially those who've been told too many times they're a problem, deserve to feel seen, not sentenced. They deserve care that believes in their best, even when they're showing us their worst.

And truthfully, so do we. As educators, we're carrying things too. And when we choose connection over control, we don't just help them... we start to heal ourselves.

This isn't about being soft. It's about being strong enough to love kids through their hard moments.

That's the kind of strength that changes lives.

## THE MEDICAL APPROACH: SEEING THE WHOLE PERSON

Imagine a student shows up to school angry. He bumps someone in the hallway. He mouths off at a teacher. He refuses to do his work.

Now pause...

Before we write him up or send him out, we should be asking, "What's going on underneath all that?"

That's the medical approach to discipline. It treats behavior like a symptom, not the whole story.

A good doctor doesn't just treat a cough. They ask questions:

- *How long has this been happening?*
- *Is it connected to something deeper, like asthma or allergies?*
- *Has the patient experienced stress, trauma, or change recently?*

Or an even deeper question about a potential family connection...***does this run in your family? What is the health of mom/dad?***

They check vital signs. They look at the bigger picture. They take time to understand, because a highly skilled doctor wants to find the root cause.

Highly skilled educators do the same. When a student is acting out, it's often because something else is going on:

- They didn't sleep last night because the house was too loud.
- They skipped breakfast and their stomach is growling.
- They're frustrated because they don't understand the lesson and are too embarrassed to ask for help.
- They're hurting from something that happened at home, in the neighborhood, or online.

The highly skilled educator might say, ***"Let me reach out to a parent/guardian to see if there is some context I do not have***."

Misbehavior is often just a loud whisper for help.

We can't keep responding to that whisper by yelling back, pushing kids away, or piling on consequences without understanding the "why" behind the "what."

## POLICING VS. MEDICAL APPROACH

*Two Ways to Respond to Student Behavior*

| | POLICING APPROACH | MEDICAL APPROACH |
|---|---|---|
| FIRST QUESTION | What rule was broken? | What happened to you? |
| FOCUS | Punishment & Control | Understanding & Healing |
| GOAL | Compliance through fear | Growth through support |
| STUDENT FEELS | Judged, defensive | Seen, heard, valued |
| CONSEQUENCE | Removal, suspension | Reflection, restoration |
| LONG-TERM OUTCOME | Resentment, resistance | Trust, accountability |
| QUESTION TO STUDENT | What is wrong with you? | What is going on with you? |

**The medical approach is to triage, to treat behavior as a symptom that needs support, not a crime that needs punishment.**

*TWO APPROACHES. TWO OUTCOMES. CHOOSE HEALING.*

## THE POLICING APPROACH: CONTROL OVER CARE

Now let's flip the lens.

The policing approach is often more about enforcing rules and handing out punishments. If a student breaks a rule, they "pay" for it; whether that's in the form of detention, in-school/out-of-school suspension, or getting sent home for a long-term suspension.. The goal here? Control is the goal. Keeping the perception of order is the goal. Showing who's in charge. It's about keeping the room quiet, instead of making sure the child is okay. It is very easily masked as 'safety', although not everything is a safety threat.

And sure, rules matter, boundaries matter. Kids need structure to feel safe. But when structure turns into surveillance, and discipline turns into punishment, we've crossed a line. We stop teaching and start policing.

It's like turning a classroom into a courtroom. The teacher becomes the judge, jury, and sometimes even the warden. Every slip-up becomes a crime. A kid talks back, and boom... they're out! A kid walks in late, boom... a write-up. There's no conversation, no curiosity, no question about what might be going on behind the behavior. Just a consequence. Just a penalty.

Ask yourself: How many kids actually come back from suspension and do better? How many come back feeling seen, heard, and supported? Many come back angrier, often shutting down, or just waving the white flag of temporary compliance. Some try to figure out a better way not to get caught or jammed up.

It's like slapping duct tape over a smoke alarm. Sure, it stops the noise, but the fire's still burning. You didn't fix anything. You just silenced it.

I had a student once.... let's call him Marcus. Every week, he was getting sent out of class. Talking too much, not sitting down, being "disrespectful." Eventually, they gave him a three-day suspension from school. When Marcus came back, nothing had changed. If anything, he was worse. Quieter, yes...but also angrier. Less trustful. I asked him what he did at home those three days.

"Played 2K," he said. "And slept."

That's not a consequence. That's a vacation. And it taught him nothing but how fast school would give up on him.

This kind of system doesn't ask, "What happened to you?" It only asks, What rule did you break? And even worse, it only cares about how fast they can get you out of sight.

The policing mindset can see kids as problems to fix or remove, not people to understand and support. That's the real issue. And when we treat students like suspects, we start to expect the worst from them. When we use specific words and language, like infraction, investigation, or suspect, there is direct messaging, whether intentional or unintentional. All of this is grooming behavior that adults are teaching and normalizing for children. Then they live up to it.

If all you carry is a hammer, every problem looks like a nail. But our kids aren't nails; they're people. They need tools, not threats. Support, not scare tactics.

## REAL-LIFE ANALOGY: THE SPRAINED ANKLE

Let's say a kid rolls their ankle in gym class. They're limping, in pain, and clearly struggling. Now picture this: instead of getting help, they're told, "You're late and disrupting class. Go sit in the hallway." Or worse, "Go home. Come back when you can walk right and move quicker, with urgency."

That sounds ridiculous, right? No decent adult would treat a physical injury that way. We'd be calling the nurse, grabbing ice perhaps, even alerting the parent. We'd understand this child needs care, not consequences.

So why do we treat emotional and behavioral struggles so differently? What is being triggered in us to respond this way?

Do we lack the skill? Do we have a deficiency in our toolkit? When you lack the tools, you can only see the nail.

When a child's hurting on the inside, we often can't see the limp. But it's there. That outburst in class might be the emotional equivalent of a sprained ankle, swollen with stress, twisted by trauma, sore from what they're carrying at home. But instead of care, too many kids get isolation, suspension, or shame.

A sprained spirit needs rest. Needs support. Needs healing. In the ways in which we would handle a twisted ankle with calm, patience, and attention, we need to handle emotional wounds with the same respect. That's the medical mindset. Not "What's wrong with you?" but "What's going on with you?" To triage.

Let's stop punishing the limp and start treating the injury.

## STUDENTS AREN'T BROKEN, THEY'RE WOUNDED

**Let's get this straight:** Our students are not broken. They're not "bad kids." They're wounded. They're human.

Some are exhausted because they didn't sleep, maybe they were up watching siblings, dodging drama, or listening to arguments through thin apartment walls. Some are walking into school carrying more than a backpack. They're carrying stress, fear, or grief, and the only way they know how to express it is through behavior that gets labeled "defiant."

But defiance is often just a mask for pain.

There was a student, we'll call her Tamia, who was always rolling her eyes and always talking back. Folks saw attitude and defiance. Her teacher saw defensiveness. One day, Tamia was asked why she was always so sharp with her words. She said, "Because grown folks are always trying to come for me, so I come first."

That's not a bad kid. That's a kid trying not to be hurt again. It is a protective defense mechanism.

See, when kids act out, it's not because they don't care. It's often because they don't know how to care for themselves in a better way yet. Most people in crisis are unable to appropriately address their needs, including adults. And that's where we come in. Not with punishment, but with purpose. Not to shut them down, but to lift them up. To teach them how to feel, how to cope, how to choose differently.

We don't excuse every behavior, but we understand it. We triage it. Then we guide them through it. That's education. That's what we signed up for. Teachers, parents, true master educators, and counselors must be committed to educating the whole child.

So, we ask:

- What does this student need?
- What can I teach them that'll stick?
- How do I reconnect, not reject?
- What support do I need as an educator from someone who is more skilled than me?

Because growth starts with connection.

## WHEN WE LEAD WITH HUMANITY, EVERYONE WINS

If we continue down the honesty road, we can say with certainty that the medical approach and adjusted mindset take more time. It takes more energy. It takes more self-work. The learning, growth, and adjustment are internal. And yes... it takes more heart.

But what it gives back is worth more than silence or control. It contributes to a school where students feel safe enough to be their true selves. Where teachers feel empowered to support growth and development, not punish. Where the culture shifts from fear to trust. Where partnership, social capital, and community thrive.

It's like the difference between a security camera and a counselor. One watches for mistakes. The other listens for pain.

When we lead and teach with humanity, classrooms become communities. Kids start to believe that their school is a place where they get invested and bought in; a place to take risks, a brave space.

We stop saying, "What's your problem?" and start saying, "You matter."

And that shift, It changes everything.

## TO TEACHERS AND STUDENTS: YOU DESERVE BETTER

**To the educators reading this:** You didn't sign up to police. You're not here just to catch kids slipping or write referrals like tickets. You're here because you believe in growth. In people. In kids who don't always get it right, but who still deserve a shot.

You are educators. You build futures, not files.

**To the students:** You are so much more than the worst thing you've done. You are not a problem to be fixed. You are a person in progress. You're learning. You're growing. And you deserve to be seen, heard, and supported, not just disciplined.

We're not here to label you. We're here to lift you.

## FINAL WORD: CHOOSE HEALING

So, here's the bottom line.

We've got a choice to make every day.

We can be the officer who writes the ticket and moves on. Or we can be the doctor who leans in and asks, "What or where does it hurt?"

We can choose to remove kids, or we can choose to reach them.

Two things can be true. Let's be the educators who check for wounds, and not just compliance. Who asks what happened, not just what rule got broken. Who builds schools that heal, not just schools that hush.

Because when we choose healing, we all rise. Students grow. Teachers thrive. And schools become what they were meant to be... places of transformation, not control centers.

Let's choose better.

Let's choose healing.

CHAPTER 05

# BE AUTHENTIC | ENERGY IS EVERYTHING

Students can sense fake energy before you even open your mouth. It's like walking into a room, and the vibe is just not right. Nobody's said anything yet, but something feels off. Maybe someone throws you a glance and a smile, but it's that kind of smile that's too big, too polished... like they practiced it in the mirror, but forgot to add the feeling behind it. Their eyes are blank, their words sound rehearsed, and their body language is stiff like they're wearing a mask they don't even like.

That's what fake can look like. You know it when you feel it.

Now picture that same energy coming from your teacher. They walk in dressed like what they *think* students want to see, using slang that expired five years ago, and making jokes that fall flat because they're trying way too hard. It's like they're playing a role, but they never got the script right. *That kind of energy*? It's heavy. It drags the whole classroom down.

Children, especially teenagers, have really sharp radars for this. They've been through enough educators to know when somebody's being real and when they're just performing. And here's the thing, most adults forget: Students don't expect perfection. They expect presence. Realness. Someone who shows up as their whole self: flaws and all.

Because truth matters. Especially in a world that keeps trying to sell you the fakeness, the goofiness, the nonsense.

At that age, our students are figuring out who they are. They're looking around at the adults in their lives, their teachers, their coaches, their parents...everybody. And whether they know it or not, they are watching the adults in their lives like a mirror. They're asking: *Is this what being grown looks like? Is this who I might become?* And if that mirror is foggy, if that adult is hiding behind a character instead of showing them their true face, the student does not get a clear reflection. And that does damage.

**One of my favorite quotes is, "People are as honest as their actions."** Authenticity isn't about being cool. It's about being consistent. Being honest. It's walking into the room and letting your energy match your intentions. *That kind of energy?* It speaks before you do. It creates trust, safety, and space for students to do the same; to be real, be open, and most importantly, vulnerable.

And when that happens, that is when actual learning begins.

So let me say this for the record, in case this is the first time or the 50th time you may be hearing this message: For every educator reading (parents included), don't try to be what you *think* students want. Just be you. Because when your energy is rooted in truth, students feel it, and they respond to it.

Let's break it down with some real-life classroom moments. Because this whole "be authentic" thing... it's not just a vibe. It shows up in what you say, how you say it, and even how you handle tough moments.

## INAUTHENTIC TEACHING: THE TRY-HARD TRAP

Let's say a teacher hears students using slang in the hallway and decides to incorporate it into their lesson, thinking it'll make them relatable. So, in the middle of explaining photosynthesis, the teacher randomly drops, "Yo, chlorophyll be lowkey clutch for the plant game."

Now, you already know how that lands. Awkward silence. Side-eyes. Maybe a couple of fake laughs out of pity. Nobody's connecting. Not because the teacher doesn't know Science, but because they're trying so hard to be "down" and connect that they forgot to be themselves. That kind of forced energy backfires. It doesn't build a bridge; it builds a wall.

The same thing happens when a teacher pretends to be unbothered by something that clearly bothers them. Like a student talks back, and instead of addressing it calmly, the teacher smiles too widely, clenches their jaw, and says in a sugar-sweet voice, "I'm not mad, everything's fine." *But the energy?* It's tight, cold, and tense. Everybody in the room feels it, and now the trust is gone. The teacher is now **disempowered. But why? Because the elephant in the room is that everyone in the room knows.**

## AUTHENTIC TEACHING: THE REAL-RECOGNIZE-REAL APPROACH

Now, picture a different teacher. They walk in, and they are not trying to perform; they are just present. Maybe they don't know all the newest slang, and they admit that upfront: "Y'all are gonna have to teach me what that means, I'm still catching up." *That honesty? That humility?* Students respect that more than a forced "cool." It shows that they are human and open.

Or maybe a student challenges the teacher in class. Instead of pretending it doesn't sting, the teacher takes a breath and says, "Hey, I hear your frustration, but I still need us to stay respectful. Let's talk it through." That's authentic. That's leadership with heart. *And students?* **They remember that. You are not the only ones giving tests, giving quizzes, and assessing mastery. Students give assessments all the time. Can you pass the authenticity test? Those who don't, struggle.**

Authentic teachers bring themselves into the room every day. They don't pretend to be perfect. They know what they know and are comfortable with what they do not know. They are honest with themselves, which is where authenticity begins. They don't hide behind some fake "teacher voice" or persona. They let students see their personality, their passions, even their mistakes. They show that it's okay to not know everything, as long as you're willing to learn, listen, and grow. They model what it looks like as an adult.

So, as the adult, **you are the model for learning. Your actions drive student buy-in. That student buy-in drives the learning.**

## QUICK SIGNS YOU'RE KEEPING IT REAL

- You admit when you don't know something, and model learning in real time.
- You talk with students, not at them. You engage in dialogue.
- You are an active listener (listening to hear vs. listening to respond).
- You stay true to your style, whether that's laid-back, energetic, serious, or silly. You learn, honor, and respect their style.
- You respect your students enough to be honest, even when it's uncomfortable.
- You listen to their feedback, even when it is uncomfortable.
- You bring consistent energy, steady, grounded, and genuine.

When teachers show up like this, students notice. They lean in. They listen. They're more likely to open up, take risks, and bring their full selves to the space. That's when an organic, authentic connection happens. That's when you stop just teaching *content* and start teaching *people*.

Because in the end, being real isn't just a classroom strategy; it's a life skill. It's a people skill. And when students see it in action, they learn to live it, too.

## FAKENESS KILLS THE VIBE

I've been in classrooms that looked perfect on the surface. The teacher had their clipboard, their learning objectives posted, and their "teacher voice" on full blast. They were so good at *doing* all of the moves. The classroom had anchor charts and posters with bright quotes like "Shoot for the moon!" and "You are capable of amazing things!" But the room felt dead. No energy, no rhythm, no connection. You could hear the ticking of the clock louder than the direct instruction. *Why?*

Because the energy wasn't real.

That teacher wasn't showing up as themselves; they were showing up as what they thought a teacher was *supposed* to look like. They were "performing education." *And that kind of staged presence?* It doesn't spark curiosity. It doesn't build trust. It doesn't make students lean in. It makes them check out.

Have you ever tried to plug your phone into a wall outlet that looks fine but doesn't actually have power? That's what it's like trying to learn from a teacher who isn't being authentic. Everything *looks* like it should work, but there's no charge. And when there's no charge, there's no connection.

*WHEN TEACHERS SHOW UP REAL, STUDENTS RESPOND IN KIND.*

## NOW LET ME SHOW YOU THE FLIP SIDE

There once was a teacher who taught in high school, Ms. Rhonda. She didn't look like your average textbook instructor. She didn't care about looking polished or following the script. What she cared about was being real and making history come alive.

Her classroom was loud; in the best way. She didn't just teach history; she lived it. She told stories like she was talking about family drama from a cookout, even if it was about wars and revolutions from centuries ago. You could tell she cared about the content, but more than that... you could tell she cared about them. She didn't wear the usual teacher clothes either. She rocked bold earrings that swayed when she moved, bright colors that matched her spirit, and sneakers so fresh it was like she walked out of a commercial.

She didn't try to be "one of her students," but she didn't try to be above them either. She met them where they were. She brought her full self into the room, and in doing that, she gave her students the permission to bring their full selves too. *That kind of energy? That kind of realness?* It was impossible to ignore. Even when they were tired or stressed or not in the mood, they showed up... because she did.

Comparatively, Mr. Pepperstine's shoe game was less than stellar. It's fair to say he met no bar in the sneaker culture or professional footwear etiquette on any level, for that matter. At that time, the staff dress code philosophy put a higher premium on instructional ability, pedagogy, and student outcomes over what teachers were wearing. Due to the flexibility of the dress code, his preferred foot dressing was an open-toe sandal or flip-flop. In fact, he was so well-known for them that students or teachers who may not have known his name could mention his feet and/or toes for an accurate description. Nonetheless, he was who he was. He took the roasts from students and staff like a champ and never wavered. Students in his classroom thrived academically and saw an educator standing "on business" even if that business was his exposed toes standing on a mere layer of fabric.

## SO, WHAT'S THE LESSON HERE?

*Authenticity isn't about being cool.* It's about being honest. I*t's about being whole.*

It's not about faking it till you make it. It's about being so comfortable in your skin that your presence tells students, *"This is a safe space. You can be you here, because I'm being me."*

That doesn't mean you have to be loud like Ms. Rhonda. You might be calm, quiet, and more of a listener. That's still real. That's still power. The point is, your power doesn't come from mimicking someone else's vibe; it comes from honoring your own.

Authenticity is magnetic. It pulls people in. It makes students feel something. And that's the key... you can't teach them anything until they feel something.

So, before you even open your mouth in the classroom, ask yourself: *What energy am I bringing in with me?*

*Because your energy?* That's the whole temperature of the room.

## WHAT DOES IT MEAN TO BE AUTHENTIC?

Being authentic means bringing you into the room: your values, your personality, your truth. That doesn't mean telling students your whole life story or making class a reality show. It means not pretending to be someone you think they'll like more.

Let's break it down. If you're not into rap music, don't start quoting Kendrick lyrics just to connect. If you've never used TikTok, don't start forcing slang you overheard in the hallway. That's not a connection, that's cosplay. And when students figure it out (because they *will*), you will lose them.

But if you love gardening? Bring in a plant and talk about how it relates to growth and patience. Do you geek out over Marvel movies or anime? Use that as a way to discuss storytelling or identity. Were you raised by your grandma, who taught you everything through food and conversation? Bring that into your teaching style.

That's your "how to." It's your blueprint. You don't need to copy anyone else's style. What you need is the courage to show up as yourself, consistently. That's what builds trust. And trust is the currency of the classroom.

## DIFFERENT STUDENTS, DIFFERENT NEEDS

Another key part of authenticity? Knowing that your students are not *one-size-fits-all.* You already know this if you've been in the game for more than a minute. What sparks one group might shut another down. What motivates Jaylen might overwhelm Maya. You can't copy-paste your approach from period to period like you're hitting "send" on an email.

Think of it like this, you are a chef. A good one. You've got the skills, the passion, and the ingredients. But every table you serve is different. Some folks want spicy, some want sweet, and some need something easy on the stomach because they've already been through too much that day. Same chef. Same kitchen. Different recipes.

**Let me give you an example.**

I had this one 3rd-period class who was rowdy, funny and full of big personalities. They needed structure like it was oxygen. So, with them, I kept my voice steady but firm. Clear routines. Quick transitions. Humor to keep things light, but always pulling the focus back in.

Now my 6th-period? a very different vibe. Quiet kids, deep thinkers, a few battling anxiety and stuff they never talked about out loud. If I came in loud with that same 3rd-period energy, I'd lose them in five minutes. With them, I lowered my voice, sat on the edge of the desk, and asked more questions than I answered. Slowed everything down. That's not being fake. That's reading the room and being *in tune*. That's the *range* (another tool).

You don't change who you are. You stretch how you are.

Some kids show up hungry for food, for attention, for safety. Some have been shouted at so much that they tune out loud voices, while others need a firm tone just to feel boundaries. Being authentic doesn't mean being the same every day; it means being *honest and flexible*, like a tree that bends in the wind but doesn't break.

The goal? Stay rooted in who you are while adjusting your reach to meet your students where they are.

## ENERGY SETS THE TONE

Let me say the thing, so it sticks: **The classroom runs on your energy. Period.**

Not your content. Not your seating chart. **You.**

Your presence is the thermostat. You walk in hot and scattered, and the room heats up with tension. You come in low-energy and disconnected? The class drifts. But when you show up grounded, eyes locked in, voice clear, body relaxed but alert, you become a calm in the middle of their storm. And believe me, some of them are walking through storms.

I remember one Monday, I came in tired. Didn't sleep well, carried the stress from home into the room. I tried to fake my way through it, but my students felt it. They weren't wild, just unsettled. Off balance. At one point, one student asked me straight up, "You good today?" I had to stop and breathe. I wasn't good, and they felt it before I even said a word.

Now flip that. On the days I come in locked in, music playing softly when they walk in, warm greeting at the door, a short story or joke to start the lesson, everything flows better. It's not magic. It's energy alignment. Students follow vibes before they follow rules.

Look, your students are watching you more than they're listening to you.

What you allow, continues. What you model spreads.

If you get snappy when you're stressed, don't be surprised when your students do the same. But if you model grace… if you say, "Hey, I'm not at 100 today, but I'm here and I'm showing up"… you're teaching resilience. You're giving them permission to be real, too.

Students don't need superheroes in front of them. They need humans who care out loud.

Be the teacher who says,

- **"I don't know, let's figure it out."**
- **"That didn't land the way I wanted; let me try again."**
- **"This topic matters to me, and I want it to matter to you, too."**

*That kind of energy?* It's contagious. And once your classroom catches it, the culture shifts. Students start asking better questions. They show each other grace. They lean into the space instead of shrinking back. They trust that showing up as themselves is enough because you modeled it first.

So, keep your energy honest. Keep it clean. Keep it intentional.

Because the real flex in education is a classroom full of students who feel safe enough to be real.

## FINAL WORD: BE THE EXAMPLE

Middle and high school students are in the thick of becoming. Every day, they're experimenting with who they are. One day, it's baggy hoodies and silence. Next, it's bold opinions and side-eyes. They're figuring out where they fit, what matters, who they can trust, and most of all, who they want to be.

And whether you realize it or not, they're watching **you** to figure that out.

Even when they won't make eye contact. Even when they're glued to their phone or pretending not to care. They're watching. Watching how you handle pressure. Watching how you speak to people who can't do anything for you. Watching whether you follow the rules you expect them to follow. Watching how you carry yourself when no one's clapping for you.

So, here's the truth:

When they see you being **real** and being **consistent**... that hits differently. That sticks.

When they see you enforce the rules with respect, even when no one's looking, you're teaching them that integrity matters. When you show up as yourself, unapologetically, without needing to fake cool or flex power, you're teaching them that identity isn't performance; it's presence. When you admit you messed up, or say, "I'm working on that too," you're showing them that being human doesn't disqualify you from being a leader; it *qualifies* you.

Because here's the thing: In a world that pressures young people to perform, to fake, to hustle for approval... your authenticity is radical. It tells them, *"You can be fully you and still be powerful. Still be respected. Still belong."*

That's what real leadership is. Not loud. Not flashy. But solid. Leading by modeling self-respect. From consistency. From the quiet confidence that doesn't need to shout to be heard.

So, ask yourself, *What example are you setting? What truth are you living out loud every time you step into the building and into that room? What kind of energy are you planting in your students that they'll carry out into the world?*

Because whatever you model, they magnify.

If you model joy, they learn that school can be a place of light. If you model boundaries with compassion, they learn that accountability can coexist with care. If you model being truly, openly, and consistently real, they learn that being themselves is enough.

That may be the most important lesson they get all year.

So, when that final bell rings and the room empties, know this: Your words matter. Your energy echoes. Your authenticity? That's the legacy. This is the foundation that builds stain. Be the example, and make it real by being authentic.

CHAPTER 06

# BUILD STAIN | HOW CREDIBLE ARE YOU?

*BUILD SOMETHING THAT STICKS. LEAVE A MARK THAT LASTS.*

Let's get into something that doesn't show up on paper, but shows up in every part of your classroom...*credibility*. Stain was mentioned in the last chapter. Your stain is your credibility. **Your authenticity builds your credibility.**

Not your degree.

Not how long you've been teaching (Maybe for adults, not for students).

Not how many trainings you've sat through or how loud they clap for you at the staff meeting.

Credibility is street-level. It's earned, not handed. It's the invisible currency that determines how far your words travel and how deep your influence goes.

See, every student who walks into your classroom is asking, "Can I trust you?" And they aren't asking it out loud. They're asking it with their body language, their eye contact, their attitude, their silence. They are studying how you engage with others and how they engage with you. And your answer to that question of trust is not in your syllabus; it's in how you carry yourself every day.

*Do your words match your actions? Do you handle your power with care, or do you flex it just because you can? Do you show up the same when the room is quiet vs when it's on fire?*

In this game, students don't care what your credentials say if your energy says something else.

We're living in a time when education is shifting fast. One year, it's block scheduling for more labs, next is more minutes. Next, it's project-based learning. The next is flipped classrooms, SEL (social emotional learning), restorative circles, or AI in the lesson plan. Every couple of months, somebody's pushing a "new" method or "new" approach as *"the answer"* to everything.

Don't get me wrong... some change is good and often necessary. However, the point here is that you can have the most cutting-edge strategies in your pocket, and if your students don't believe in you, it won't matter. They will not buy-in and will not follow where you're trying to lead them.

**Let me say that again:** *If students don't believe in you, they won't believe in what you're teaching.*

It's like trying to give somebody water in a dirty glass. You might have something life-giving in your hands, but if the container ain't clean, if your actions don't match your message, they're not going to drink it. And honestly, you can't blame them. Would you?

## CREDIBILITY ≠ CREDENTIALS

You might have the degrees. You might have the plaques, the certifications, the binders full of perfectly aligned standards... and that's fine. I applaud you. We all do. That's not what students are watching.

- They're watching whether your tone shifts depending on who you are talking to.
- They're watching how you respond when they mess up.
- They're watching how you talk about students when you think they're not listening.

**Because credibility doesn't speak to content...it's aligned to character.**

It's about whether you do what you say you'll do. Whether you treat them like human beings. Whether you bring that same energy on a rainy Monday in February that you had on the first week of school.

**Here's a story for you:**

Malik was a quiet kid. He didn't cause problems, but didn't say much either. A lot of teachers overlooked him. Just another name on the roster. But every day, his teacher greeted him at the threshold by name. Asked how he was doing. Didn't press, just stayed consistent. Weeks went by, no change. Then one day, out of nowhere, Malik says to his teacher, "You really mean that when you ask, don't you?"

That hit his teacher.

He wasn't testing his teacher's knowledge, but rather their consistency. Testing if they were really who they said they were.

That's credibility. That's what builds trust. Not the flash. Not the performance.

Just the daily decision to show up real.

So, when we talk about "Build Stain," we're talking about the kind of presence that *sticks*. That leaves a mark. That becomes part of your students' internal compass long after they've left your classroom.

## Ī BĒFORE Ē

You don't have to be perfect.

You just have to be real.

You don't have to have every answer.

You just have to be honest.

You don't have to entertain. You just have to care.

Say what you mean. Mean what you say, and let your expectations come from care, not control. Because when students feel that? When they know you're solid, even on your off days... that's when they give you access to who they really are; and that's where the real teaching begins.

## "BUILD STAIN" | LEAVE A MARK THAT LASTS

Have you ever spilled something on a white T-shirt and no matter what detergent you use, hot water, cold water, bleach, it stays? It doesn't matter how many times you wash it, it leaves its mark. That's what credibility does when it's real. It stains. Not in a negative way, but in a permanent way. A lasting way. It's not surface-level like a motivational poster. It's deep. Soaked in. Absorbed. Like a tattoo.

That's the kind of educator you want to be. The kind that doesn't just show up for the job, but one who leaves something behind in the student's memory long after the bell rings, long after the school year ends. You aren't trying to be a temporary presence. You're trying to be a permanent influence. A reference point.

"Build stain" means make it stick. Students won't always remember the worksheet you handed out or the exact words you used in your lecture. But they'll remember:

- That you looked them in the eye when they were struggling.
- That you didn't give up on them after they gave you attitude.
- That you celebrated them in ways that felt personal, not performative.
- That you protected them when nobody else did.

They'll remember that you stayed solid.

See, kids test adults. Not because they're trying to break us, but because they're trying to figure out which adults won't break *on them.* They want to know:

- Can I trust you when I'm at my lower self?
- Will you still treat me with dignity when I mess up?
- Are you going to be the same today as you were last week?

They're not just watching for discipline. They're watching for emotional consistency.

Because in their world, where family might be unstable, where social media shows people switching up and clout-chasing, where trust is rarely kept, they are craving someone they don't have to second-guess.

They don't need a superhero. They need someone who won't fold under pressure. Someone who doesn't switch up when the class gets loud or when they don't immediately respond the way you wanted. **Someone who can teach them what it looks like to do it the right way.**

Our youth today are dealing with things many of us weren't facing when we were their age. Some are raising younger siblings. Some are translating for their parents. Some are dodging real trauma, violence, poverty, depression, at a magnified level, and they are still showing up to school like everything's cool. But underneath that tough shell? They're watching. Not for perfection, but for proof that you care.

Care doesn't mean being soft. It means being present. It means knowing your students well enough to see who's slipping through the cracks before they hit the floor. It means not confusing silence with compliance. It means recognizing that every child isn't testing you to be disrespectful... some are just checking your temperature to see what you look like when things get messy.

**So, Build That Stain.**

Leave something behind that they can carry. Not just your rules. Not just your routines. But your presence. Your *integrity*. Your *truth*. Let your impact show up years later when they're in a tough spot. They'll remember something you said, or better yet, something you didn't say but showed with your actions.

They don't need you to be perfect. They need you to be etched into their growth.

When we say "build stain," we're saying be the kind of teacher who doesn't get washed out of memory. Not because you were the funniest, or the most decorated, but because you were *real*... and you were *there*. Every day. Every student. Every time.

That's the stain that stays. And that's what changes lives.

## WHAT DOES CREDIBILITY LOOK LIKE IN ACTION?

Let's pull this out of theory and into the room... your room. *"Credibility"* can sound big and abstract, but in reality, it shows up in the small stuff. The daily stuff. The decisions you make when nobody's clapping. Your decisions minus the *"at-a-boys,"* or the *"hey look at me(s)."*

You might not even notice it happening in real time. But your students do.

Let me give an example: There was this young girl named Aaliyah.

She was in the eighth grade. Smart, sharp, and had a quiet strength about her. But she also came with a short fuse and a thick emotional wall. Teachers had labeled her as "difficult." If you have been teaching for some time, you are familiar with a version of this scenario. They say, *"She's got potential, but she needs an attitude check."*

In the first week of school, Aaliyah walks in late. She doesn't explain; doesn't apologize. Just slides into her seat with headphones halfway in. Her new teacher, given the reputation they had been told about Aaliayah, could have snapped. They could have sent her out or written her up to show the class that they meant business. But instead, her new teacher paused. They said to her, "Good to see you. Glad you're here. Let me know if you need to catch up." That's it. They didn't press her. They didn't scold her. Checked in after class in private, with little to no response.

That moment? That was a seed. A test. She didn't say much back. But the next day? She came in on time. No headphones. Still quiet, but she looked her teacher in the eye.

A few weeks later, Aaliyah's teacher found out that she was bouncing between her mom's place and her aunt's. No steady ride to school. Waking up early to help get her little brother dressed. Still showing up. Still doing the work.

**Here's the point:** Credibility happened not because her new teacher "handled" her, but because they didn't try to control her. They created space. They stayed consistent. They didn't judge her story based on what they heard about her beforehand, yet they hadn't given her a chance to explain. From that moment on, Aaliyah and her teacher's relationship changed. Not overnight, but piece by piece. She started participating more in class. She started asking questions, and turning in work with detail. Not because her new teacher demanded it, but because that teacher had earned her trust. That's credibility. That's what stain looks like in action.

## REFLECTION: WHAT KIND OF MARK ARE YOU LEAVING?

So, take a moment. Think back to your week.

- Was there a moment you could've reacted but chose to respond with **care** instead?
- Was there a student testing your patience who might really be testing your **consistency?**
- Are there students who seem distant but might be waiting to see if your energy is **safe?**

Credibility isn't built in grand gestures. It's *built in moments like those.*

Every choice you make in front of your students tells them something about you. Every tone, every pause, every "good morning," every time you choose patience instead of power...it all adds up.

So, ask yourself daily: "Am I building something that sticks? Or something that gets washed away?" Because the stain you leave, good or bad, is the part of you that walks out the door with them.

## HOW TO BUILD CREDIBILITY DAILY

These aren't big, dramatic gestures. These are small, intentional choices, coupled with consistency that add up over time. The kind that builds trust, respect, and classroom culture, for real.

- Say their name, and say it right. Respect starts with identity. Students feel seen when you get their name right and use it consistently.
- Greet every student, even if they don't greet you back. Your "Hello" might be the only positive and respectful acknowledgment they get all day. Keep showing up.
- Be where you say you'll be. If you promise to check in, follow up. Under promise and over deliver, not vice versa. If you say, "I'll grade that tonight," then do it, or own it if you don't.

## CREDIBILITY CHECKLIST:

1. **Hold everyone to the same standard, including yourself.** Don't let one student slide just because they're easy to manage, or go hard on another just because they push back. Be fair. Be even.
2. **Respond, don't react.** Take a breath before you discipline. Ask questions. Stay calm. A calm adult calms the room.
3. **Apologize when you mess up.** This is big. If you lose your cool, make the wrong call, or misjudge a situation... own it. Students will respect it.
4. **Show your human side.** Share your hobbies, your humor, your background (when appropriate). Let students know you're a real person, not just a title.
5. **Follow through with care, not control.** When you set a boundary, explain the why. Show them that discipline and dignity can live in the same space.
6. **Check in without calling out.** "You good?" in a quiet moment can go further than a public callout. Watch how you approach correction... it matters.
7. **Be consistent. Same energy.** Every day(most days). Even when you're tired. Even when the lesson flops. Show up steady; it builds safety.

Building credibility isn't about being flawless; it's about being faithful to what you say and who you are.

Every day is a brick. Every moment is mortar. Keep laying that foundation. Because students don't need perfect. They need real.

## CREDIBILITY IS A SAFE SPACE

Your classroom should feel like a place where students can finally exhale.

Not because it's perfect. Not because it's quiet. But because it's safe. **Because it's CLEAN, kept, cared for, tended to.** Safe to be themselves. Safe to make mistakes. Safe to not have the answer right away.

*And that safety?* It doesn't start with rules or routines, it starts with you. It starts when students know you're going to show up the same way every day. Not high-energy one day and checked out the next. Not warm one week and cold the next.

*Consistent.*

*Present.*

*Solid.*

For many students, especially those carrying trauma or instability, predictability feels like protection. If they know how you're going to respond, if they know you'll correct them with compassion, not humiliation, they feel like they can breathe. And breathing? That's the first step toward learning.

Some students walk through school like they're wearing armor. Not because they want to, but because they've had to. They've learned not to trust adults who say one thing and do another. They've learned to stay guarded. So, when you create a space where they can *take that armor off*, even for a period or two a day... that's powerful. That's healing.

And it goes beyond lesson plans.

Being present in a student's life outside the lesson is worth more than a hundred slide shows, colorful charts, or animated GIFs.

No, you can't show up for everything. Nobody's asking for miracles. But that one time you show up at a game, popping in during lunch, walking through during recess, or in an enrichment class (Art, P.E.)? That moment you check in after they've experienced a rough night or morning? That quiet word in the hallway saying, *"I see you. You good?"*...that stuff lands deeper than you think.

One of the teachers that I was mentoring told me a story once about having a student who was failing two classes and barely speaking in either class. That teacher went to the student's poetry showcase after school. The teacher sat in the back. Didn't say much, just clapped when the student was done. The next day, that student turned in her first full assignment of the semester.

That's not a coincidence. That's stain. That's credibility. Those moments are the ones they carry.

## YOUR CREDIBILITY BUILDS THEIR CHARACTER

When students know you're credible, when it's not just something you say, but something you live, the whole atmosphere changes. Something shifts in them. I know some educators who may have taught students in elementary school, middle school, or even high school underclassmen who show up to graduations and promotional ceremonies for their former students when possible, still showing up with tears of joy and love.

You'll notice they start to self-correct. Not because they're scared of you, but because they respect the space you've created. They won't always tell you, but they start making different choices because they don't want to break that trust you've built.

They ask more questions; not because they're trying to impress you, but because they trust you'll answer without making them feel small. They start putting in effort; not because you're watching, but because they know you care enough to notice.

And then you start seeing growth that isn't in your teacher evaluation checklist:

- That quiet student who used to hide in the back? Now they're leading a group project.
- That kid who acted too cool for school? Now they're asking, *"What can I do to pull this grade up?"*

- That student who used to be all sharp edges and side-eyes? Now they're smiling more. Relaxing. Breathing.

That's not classroom management. That's relationship leadership. That's what credibility does, it shifts the culture, not just the behavior.

This isn't about being your students' best friend. It's about being the adult they can count on. You don't have to entertain. You don't have to be trendy. You just have to be *present, respectful, and real.* Every day. Every student. Every time.

## SO...HOW CREDIBLE ARE YOU?

Let's flip the mirror for real.

Ask yourself:

- Do your students know your word means something?
- Do they feel protected in your room, or judged?
- Do they know you'll show up for them even when it's not convenient?
- Do you give them space to mess up, and still believe they can bounce back?

Credibility isn't about control. It's about care with consistency. It's about the way you teach, the way you listen, the way you show students they matter, even when nobody's watching. And no, you don't have to be perfect. That's not what they need. They need to be steady. They need to be safe. They need authenticity.

When students believe you, they start believing in themselves. *And that belief?* That's what turns discipline into growth. That's what turns resistance into buy-in. That's what transforms a classroom into a community.

So yeah... ask yourself one more time: *How credible are you?*

Because that answer shapes *everything*. More than the lesson plan. More than the test scores.

That answer is the one they carry long after your class is over.

# BUILDING CREDIBILITY DAILY

*Actions That Build Stain*

- ☑ **Say their name**, and say it right
- ☑ **Greet every student**, even if they don't greet you back
- ☑ **Be where you say you'll be**
- ☑ **Hold everyone to the same standard** (including yourself)
- ☑ **Respond**, don't react
- ☑ Apologize when you mess up
- ☑ **Show your human side**
- ☑ Follow through with care, not control
- ☑ Check in without calling out
- ☑ Be consistent - same energy, every day

*ACTIONS THAT BUILD CREDIBILITY. ONE DAY AT A TIME.*

CHAPTER 07

# VOICE (THE POWER OF THE SPOKEN WORD)

The saying, "teaching is a lot," is an understatement. Between the lesson planning and internalization, stacks and stacks of work to grade, endless meetings, parent follow-ups, and keeping up with ever-changing standards, it can feel like we're constantly playing catch-up. But underneath all of that, there's something just as important we can't afford to overlook: our voice. Not just the way we explain fractions or assign essays, but in the tone we set. That voice, the way we speak about our students when they are not in the room, the stories we choose to

tell. Our voice holds power. It creates the emotional undercurrent of our classrooms. It tells students, whether we mean to or not, what kind of people we believe they can become. So, let's pause and really ask: Why do our students' voices matter? The answer isn't just philosophical; it's practical, urgent, and real. Because if students don't learn how to speak up, advocate, question, and express themselves while they are with us, when will they learn how to speak up? The world they are stepping into doesn't reward silence. It demands boldness. It demands clarity, and it is our job to show them how to build that courage, not just by telling them they have a voice, but by demonstrating what it means to use their voice with integrity.

Think about the phrase, "One band, one sound." It's more than just a catchy line from a movie. It is a truth about what it means to work as one. In a band, if one musician is out of sync, the entire performance suffers. The same applies to our schools. Our words, actions, our tone, even the way we talk about students in the teachers' lounge, echoes. We are either lifting the culture or tearing it down.

We are not just individuals teaching isolated subjects. We are part of a collective; voices that together can uplift or discourage, include or exclude. And students are watching. Closely. They take their cues from us. If we model compassion, they learn empathy. If we speak up for fairness, they begin to understand justice. If we own our mistakes and speak with humility, they learn that strength includes vulnerability.

## LET ME TELL YOU ABOUT JORDAN.

Jordan was quiet. Smart, observant, but always at the edge of the room. He was the kind of student who completed assignments without complaint, but never raised his hand. Never volunteered. For weeks, his teacher assumed Jordan was just shy. But one day, during a class discussion on community issues, his teacher asked the students to write anonymously about something they would change in their neighborhood if they had the power. Even though Jordan's paper was written anonymously, it stopped his teacher cold. It was raw, honest, full of frustration,

and full of vision. Jordan had written about how the city ignored the park in his part of town, how broken lights and trash made kids feel forgotten. He ended with, "If no one sees us, how are we supposed to believe we matter?"

That was the moment his teacher realized Jordan wasn't shy. He just hadn't been invited to speak in a way that felt safe or real. Jordan's teacher decided to do something different. He shared Jordan's words with the class, anonymously at first, and asked the students for their ideas. The room lit up. Then, with some encouragement, Jordan spoke. For the first time, his voice filled the room. He had ideas; real ones. The class rallied around his ideas. That discussion turned into a letter-writing campaign. That campaign turned into a student-led proposal. And that proposal? It earned the attention of a local council member. A year later, the park was renovated.

Jordan's voice mattered. It always had. He just needed someone to help him believe it. That's what we are here for as educators. Being the example in your classroom is not about being perfect. It's about being intentional.

Use your voice to model what purpose-driven speech looks like: words that heal instead of harm. Use your voice to challenge rather than shame, spark rather than silence. When we lead with that kind of voice, our students will begin to trust their own voice. And once they do, they won't just speak, they will lead.

## THE POWER OF VOICE (WEAPON OR A TOOL)

Words hold weight. Heavyweight. They can build a child up or tear them down before they even know what hit them. They can spark something. They can ignite the voice of a student who has been sitting in silence. At the same time, they can shut the whole thing down with just a look and a wrong tone. I've seen it both ways. I've done it both ways. And honestly, so have many of you. It's not just what we said; it's how we said it. That tone you carry, that energy you walk into the room with...it matters. Students don't just hear your words. They feel them. They're reading your face, your posture, your pauses. You might think you're just being firm, but if your voice is laced with disappointment or sarcasm, they hear that louder than the words themselves.

Take a student like Devon. Math wasn't his strength, and he often felt like he couldn't keep up. One day, after failing a quiz, a teacher pulled him aside, looked him in the eye, and said, "Don't let this number define you. I see how hard you work. That matters more than you know." That simple sentence? It stayed with Devon. He didn't suddenly ace every test, but he walked a little taller. He started to believe he was capable. He felt seen.

Now contrast that with another moment, a different student, a different class. A teacher, fed up and frustrated, told a student, "You're smart, but you've got too much attitude. You're never gonna get far with that chip on your shoulder." The words were sharp, the tone dismissive. The student shut down. Stopped speaking. Stopped trying. That's the kind of impact the wrong tone can have, it shuts the door before the conversation even starts.

So, I say this to every educator reading these words: Your voice is your instrument. You can use it to build trust, to create a rhythm of respect in your classroom, or you can use it to cut, sometimes without even meaning to. But once those words are out, you can't pull them back.

And our kids? Especially our Black and Brown kids? They've already heard too many voices telling them they are not enough. Let your voice be the one that tells them differently. Speak like they matter, because they do. Speak like they're full of potential, because they are. And speak like you've been in their shoes, because some of us have, and the rest need to start trying.

Don't underestimate your power. A sentence can stay with a child for life. Make sure the one they remember from you is the one that lifts. This is the call: your voice is your instrument. Use it to build, to uplift, to guide because students remember how you made them feel; not just for a quarter, a semester, but for life.

## TEACHING STUDENTS THE VALUE OF THEIR VOICE

One of the most important things we can teach our students, especially those who have been overlooked, underestimated, or spoken over, is that their voice matters. That truth alone can change the trajectory of a young person's life. But knowing your voice matters is only the beginning. We have to guide them in learning how to use it, why it matters, and when to speak, even when it's uncomfortable.

It's about more than participation points or answering questions in class. It's about raising their hand to say, "That's not right," when someone's being treated unfairly. It's about having the courage to ask for help when they're struggling instead of suffering in silence. It's about speaking up for a friend, leading a group with confidence, or simply learning to express what they feel instead of bottling it up.

Take a student like Kyla. She barely spoke during the first semester of school. She always sat in the back, kept her eyes on her notebook, and rarely looked up when questions were asked. She wasn't disruptive, but she also never engaged. Her teachers could tell she had something to say, something inside her trying to push through, but the opportunity never quite felt right. One day, her teacher assigned her a role in a group project in which she would need to pitch her team's idea to the class. At first, she hesitated. She quietly said, "I'm not good at talking."

But her teacher responded gently, "That's not true. You've just never been given enough space to prove otherwise." She practiced. Rehearsed after school. The day of the presentation, her hands were shaking. Her voice wobbled. But when she finished, the class clapped; not politely, but genuinely. You know what happened after that? She started speaking up more. She started believing in her voice. That moment wasn't just about the project; it was about her learning that when she speaks, people listen. Our job is to build those moments on purpose. Create spaces where students feel safe enough to speak and brave enough to keep doing it. Their voice isn't just noise; it's necessary.

*THEIR VOICES MATTER. WHEN WE LISTEN, THEY LEAD.*

## THE COLLECTIVE STUDENT VOICE

That necessity was evident back on April 27th, 2016, during a high school student protest. There were some significant staffing changes being made that year with a direct, lasting impact on students. Several students felt some of the changes were decided in a vacuum, uninformed, and not in the best interest of students. Students reached out informally to staff members they knew and trusted, with no real response or explanation that was satisfactory. Some students, including student council members, decided to organize a sit-in on a testing day to demand that the collective voice of students be heard. Control was a non-factor. I'm sure most adults would have preferred students to comply with the ask to return to classes for testing and get some sort of follow-up at a later time, explaining how change can be difficult but necessary. And how this is a learning opportunity for students. This was more than uncomfortable for adults in and out of the building, me included.

Students demanded time and dialogue with the decision-makers to lift their voices into the space and advocate for some 'say' in what the next steps would be. What was extremely illuminating for the adults was the students' "Why." It was a perspective that was not considered, and more frankly, taken for granted. Some of the outcomes from that day included a shift in hiring, with some students lending feedback on prospective teachers. Some teachers' jobs were spared from termination based on student impact. The student body and adults were able to see what effective agency looks like in action. It was a showing of strong, organized, solid resistance in service of progressive change. It has been one of the more impactful experiences for me in all my years of education. That experience for me as a learner has shaped how I approach the work as an educator, leader, key stakeholder, and decision maker. It has also impacted how I manage directly, peer to peer, and manage up. Ask anyone!

## LEADING BY EXAMPLE

Our students learn more from what we do than what we say. They are

watching us like hawks. They hear our tone, see how we handle tension, and notice if we treat each question with respect or impatience. And they're taking notes.

If we want them to value their voice, we need to show them what it looks like to use one with dignity and intention. That means checking ourselves, because yes, we are tired. Yes, the job is hard. But no, that's not a license to speak carelessly. Some of us are decorated with degrees on our walls and years in the game. However, that doesn't excuse a tone that wounds or words that dismiss.

Take a teacher named Ms. Carter. She had a sharp student named Marcus.

inquisitive, but often pushing boundaries. Marcus wasn't afraid to challenge what didn't make sense to him, and he didn't always wait his turn to do it. One day, in the middle of a lesson, he interrupted her for the third time. Frustrated, Ms. Carter snapped and said, "Marcus, if you think you know more than the teacher, maybe you should be up here." Marcus's expression changed immediately. He sank into his seat and didn't speak again for the rest of the week. Ms. Carter could feel it; she had closed a door, and that door might not open again so easily. So, a few days later, she pulled Marcus aside and said, "I was frustrated, and I let it show. That wasn't the right way to handle it. You have a sharp mind, and I should have treated that with more care."

That apology wasn't easy. But it mattered. From that day forward, Marcus started contributing again. This time with more thoughtfulness, not less. He respected Ms. Carter more because he saw her take responsibility for her actions.

We can't model respectful dialogue if we are above admitting when we get it wrong. We can't ask students to communicate with empathy if we lead with ego. Every student walks into our classrooms carrying more than we can see: history, pride, trauma, resistance. If we don't speak to that with care, we risk sending a message that only some voices count.

This is not reserved for big moments only. One time, a teacher shut down a student's honest question with a quick, "Didn't you read the directions?" The class went silent. The student's shoulders dropped, and they didn't speak again for the rest of the period. Later, a colleague reminded that teacher, gently but firmly: "Every question is a risk. If we shut one down, it might be the last one we ever hear from that student."

Bottom line: our voices teach more than our lesson plans ever will. Let's make sure what we are teaching is worth remembering. A counter response from a student to that teacher's comment can also be one of malice and vulgarity. This is another voice of students, at times triggered by adults. That voice typically leads to more punitive responses, often justified by the impact of disrespect to the adult. We must be mindful of the power of our voices as well as our student voices.

## CREATING A CULTURE OF UNITY

Unity among educators is more than a buzzword; it's a lifeline. When we, as teachers, paraprofessionals, office staff, counselors, administrators, and even parents, move in sync, we hold each other accountable to a shared standard of tone, respect, and purpose. Our students feel that strength. More importantly, they trust it.

Our kids are watching us: watching how we speak to each other in the hallway, watching how we back each other up or don't. Watching how we correct in love instead of embarrassment, how we share praise, how we model patience when it's not easy. They soak all of that in. When they see us standing together, they feel safe enough to stand on their own.

I know of a school where they held monthly "unity huddles"...just fifteen minutes at the end of the week where all of the staff circled up and checked in. They shared highs and lows. Lifted each other. Re-centered. It wasn't fancy. But its reminder was a reflection on togetherness. And you better believe that energy made its way into their classrooms. That's what happens when we lead with one voice.

## THE POWER OF THE TONGUE

There's a reason our elders quoted the biblical Proverb that says, "Death and life are in the power of the tongue."(Proverbs 18:21) That's not just scripture, it's truth. Words shape worlds. A careless comment can plant doubt so deep it takes years to dig out. But a single sentence, spoken with care, conviction, and truth, can

unlock something in a child that no test score ever will.

As African American educators, Latinx, Asian, or other minority educators, some of us carry a sacred legacy. Our words have always mattered because, for generations, they were all we had. When our ancestors were denied access, denied fairness, denied dignity, it was the word, whether spoken, sung, or preached. It was passed down, and that kept us going. That legacy lives in us, and it calls us to use our voice with purpose.

I've had students walk into my classroom, into my school building, carrying the weight of the world. And I've learned that sometimes, all it takes is one line to start turning it around: "I believe in you." "I'm glad you're here." "You matter to me." That could very well be the only inspirational, asset-based voice that a student hears all day. Don't underestimate those words. One of my former principals, close colleague, and friend, Kevin Brown, would tell students, "I love you all," during assemblies. I was always humbled and motivated by his approach and the way he used his voice intentionally.

## ONE VOICE, ONE MESSAGE

Let this be our charge: that we move with one voice, not uniformity, but unity. That we speak with one message: not just in what we say, but in how we show up.

That message is this: You belong. You matter. You are enough, and we see you.

Let that echo from every hallway, every classroom, every conversation until our students not only hear it but believe it themselves. Because when they do, their own voices will rise. Together, we'll build something stronger than a classroom... we'll build a strong community.

One voice. One message. One purpose.

Let's be that voice.

CHAPTER 08

# CHOICES & CONSEQUENCES RESPECT THE PROCESS

*EVERY CHOICE IS A CHANCE TO GROW. EVERY CONSEQUENCE, A LESSON.*

## Ī BĒFORE Ē

Choices and consequences go hand in hand. However, they are not the same thing. This has been an unpopular opinion, especially for some educators without children. As educators, we have a responsibility to know the difference and to handle both with wisdom, not just reaction.

It's easy to fall into the trap of thinking a student is their mistake, as if one bad decision tells the whole story of who they are. But that couldn't be further from the truth. A poor choice doesn't define a child any more than any of us who have made some egregious mistakes as children and adults. In many cases, it is a indicative of a moment of confusion, pressure, inexperience, or immaturity. In many cases, that decision may be the first time they've faced a situation like that, and they simply didn't have the tools to respond effectively. When it is a repeated decision, that's evidence that no learning has occurred from the last instance.

Sometimes, students act without fully understanding that there are other options. What may seem like a clear right or wrong to us might not have been so obvious from where they stand. This is especially true for students navigating complex emotions, difficult home lives, or past trauma. Their lens is different; sometimes cloudy, sometimes cracked. And if we are not careful, we judge the action without understanding the context (judging...aligned to the policing approach in chapter 4).

That's why our response as educators is just as important as the student's original choice. A consequence should be more than a reaction. It should be part of a learning process. It is the experience that creates an opportunity for the student reflect, understand, and grow. If all we offer is punishment, without purpose or guidance, then we haven't really taught anything. We may have interrupted behavior for the moment, but we have not addressed the root cause or helped the student make a better choice next time.

In short, if the consequence doesn't teach, it doesn't serve.

### MISTAKES | NOT THE WHOLE STORY

As you read this book and reflect on your own practice, mistakes made are likely glaring and flashing in your mind like a 'road work ahead' sign. Just like some of us adults, students are still learning how to be human. They are still figuring out how to process emotions, how to read a room, and how to hold themselves accountable. Some of them are carrying trauma we couldn't even begin to imagine. As adults, we have the financial means and access to formal therapeutic support. Some of them are reacting, not deciding. That's why we can't let a single moment define them in our eyes. We can't freeze-frame a bad choice and use it as the headline for who they are.

Let's say a student mouths off in class. They are loud and disrespectful. The energy shifts, and everybody's watching. You feel yourself getting tight, ready to lay down the law. But before you do, pause.

*Ask yourself:*

- **What was behind that outburst?**
- **Have I seen this student struggle before?**
- **Am I mad because it was rude, or because it made me look bad?**

It's okay to be human and feel disrespected, but don't let your pride write the consequence. That's not growth. That's payback. The growth is avoiding internalizing the negative response. If you truly ask the question, the correct response will present itself in the process.

## THE PROCESS IS THE POINT

**Here's the thing:** students often learn more from the process than the punishment, and so do we. So, ask yourself, how can this consequence teach? What can this consequence teach?

If a student cheats, don't just hit them with a zero and call it a day. That might make your gradebook feel cleaner, but it leaves the lesson behind. Instead, have a one-on-one with the student. Ask them what led to the choice they made. Did they feel overwhelmed? Was it pressure from home? Then make the consequence fit the growth: redo the assignment, write a reflection, or meet with a tutor. Make them work for it, but make it mean something.

Real consequences guide. They restore. They give a student a way back, not just a traditional disconnected transaction, or a mental slap on the wrist.

## KNOW THE DIFFERENCE BETWEEN A MISTAKE AND A PATTERN

There's an important line between offering grace and enabling behavior, and as educators, we have to know where that line is. Showing understanding doesn't mean letting everything slide. It means being thoughtful. It means taking the time to look at the 'why' behind the behavior, not just the behavior itself.

You have to know your students. That takes time and effort. Not just their names and their grades, but how they carry themselves, what they're dealing with outside of school, and what their triggers might be. That kind of knowledge can only come through building relationships. When you take the time to learn who a student really is, you can better recognize the difference between a one-time slip and a developing pattern.

Let's take two students, both of whom skip class. One skips for the first time. You check in and find out they were feeling overwhelmed. Maybe they are juggling responsibilities at home, or maybe just trying to get a mental break. The other student has skipped three times this week and has no problem telling everyone how they don't care about school. Same action. Different reasons. Falls under the same rule, but absolutely requires a different response. This is where discernment comes in. It's easy to rely on blanket consequences: give everyone the same punishment, write the referral, mark the absence, move on. But that approach lacks humanity. It doesn't account for context. It doesn't challenge us to dig deeper and ask the hard questions about what our students need to change course.

Real teaching happens when we use our authority with empathy. When we recognize that consistency doesn't mean sameness, it means fairness. And fairness takes work. It requires thought. It requires an equity lens. It demands that we show up not just as instructors, but as people who care about the lives we are shaping.

When a student messes up, take a pause.

*Ask yourself:*

- **Is this a one-time misstep or part of a bigger pattern?**
- **What support does this student need to make better choices?**
- **What kind of consequence will push them toward growth, not just compliance?**

We are not just here to enforce rules. We are here to help students learn how to live within them and grow beyond them.

## A STORY ABOUT THE PROCESS

Let's talk about a student named Tyrell. He was bright, full of energy, and quick with his words. Equally, his temper was just as quick. One day, during group work, a classmate said something slick, and Tyrell exploded. He threw his chair back, cursed, and stormed out. Immediate reaction from most people would have been suspension, no questions asked. But his teacher, Mr. Lawson, didn't go there first. Instead, he took a pause. He let Tyrell cool off, then sat down with him after school. Mr. Lawson asked Tyrell, straight up, "What happened?"

Tyrell explained he was already having a rough morning. He disclosed how his little sister had been crying all night, his mom left for her overnight shift without saying goodbye, and he hadn't eaten since the day before. He was tired. He was hungry. When the other student came at him sideways, it lit a fuse within him.

Mr. Lawson listened. He didn't excuse the behavior, but he made the consequence match the moment. He had Tyrell write a letter to the class about what respect looks like and why it matters. Tyrell also had to meet with the school counselor twice that week. The facilities manager, with assistance from Tyrell, reset the room he had disrupted.

Was it a consequence? Yes. But it was also growth. Tyrell owned his actions. He learned from them. And most importantly, he saw that his teacher didn't give up on him in the moment he lost control.

## CHECK YOURSELF BEFORE YOU WRECK THAT RELATIONSHIP

Sometimes, the issue in the classroom isn't the student. Oftentimes, the issue is us adults. Have you ever found yourself frustrated with the same student, over and over? Its the one whose name keeps popping up on referrals. It's the name that always has the chats buzzing. It's the one who is known by most adults by that full government (first/last) name. It's that student you brace for before they even walk in the room. Pause and think about that. Have you stopped seeing them as a developing young person? Have you started seeing them as a problem instead of a possibility?

When that happens, it's not just about classroom management anymore. It's about our mindset, and we owe it to our students to check that mindset regularly. Because if we're being honest, some educators walk into school buildings with unchecked biases or unresolved frustration unconsciously, quite often. Sometimes that shows up as low expectations. Other times, it shows up as anger masked as authority. And the worst part is It can be easily normalized. People reframe it as tough love or being strict, when really...it is resentment dressed up as professionalism.

When you are more invested in punishing a student than in helping them grow,

that's not education, that's retaliation. That means you've stopped seeing the child and started protecting your pride, your ego, and that says more about us as adults than it does about the students we serve.

Teaching requires emotional maturity. When we respond from a place of anger, frustration, or ego, we lose the very power we are supposed to model. It becomes less about guidance and more about control. Our students, whether they admit it or not, can feel that shift.

If you find yourself emotionally charged, take a step back. Pause. Breathe. Write it down, talk it out, or sleep on it. Ask a trusted colleague for perspective. Because in those moments when your emotions are loud, your wisdom can go quiet.

Discipline should come from clarity, not heat. From purpose, not pride. If we want students to take responsibility for their actions, we have to model what it looks like to take responsibility for ours. In the end, every choice we make in how we handle behavior shapes the classroom culture. Will it be a space for punishment, or a space for growth? Will students leave your room feeling pushed down or pulled forward? That's the power we hold, and we need to handle it with care.

## CHOICES SHOULD LEAD TO GROWTH

If we truly believe education is about learning, then we have to make room for our students to make mistakes, real ones, without letting those mistakes define them. Our classrooms should be spaces where students can say, Yeah, I messed up, and still be welcomed back into the process of becoming better. That's not lowering expectations; that's raising the standard for how we build character, how to build advocacy.

Every student needs to know that growth is possible; not just for the straight A-student or the compliant ones who behave perfectly, but for the ones who stumble, who test limits, who act out when they don't know how to ask for help. If we want students to learn from their choices, we have to give them a path back. When a student feels boxed in by their past mistakes, they start to believe there are no choices and there's no point in trying to change.

That's why the consequences we give must reflect more than a rulebook. They should reflect our belief in that student's future. Let your consequences be mirrors that help students reflect on who they are and who they could be. Don't let them become walls that block their path forward. When we focus only on the punishment, we often miss the chance to support the real change.

It's also worth remembering that we are shaping far more than a grade point average. We are shaping how a young person sees themselves in moments of failure. Do they see someone who made a mistake and can recover? Or do they see someone who is now permanently labeled, diminished, and defined by their worst day? That perception follows them. It travels home. It carries into their next classroom. It walks with them into adulthood. So, what do you want your students to remember about you? How you responded when they messed up? Did you hold the line and hold the door open? Did you address the behavior, but also remind them they were still worthy of learning, growing, and belonging?

That is the heart of teaching. It's not just about helping students get things right. It's about walking with them when they get it wrong and showing them how to find their way back.

Being a real educator means checking your ego at the door. It means seeing discipline as an opportunity, not a battleground. It means remembering that we are here to build up, not break down.

The next time a student makes a poor choice, remember this:

- The consequence should connect to the behavior.
- The student should be part of the reflection.
- And you should be part of the solution.

Respect the process. Because when we do that, we teach them how to own their choices, learn from them, and come out stronger on the other side.

One choice. One consequence. One opportunity to grow.

CHAPTER 09

# TEACHING VS. PARENTING STYLES
# KNOW YOUR ROLE

There's a clear difference between being a parent in the classroom and being a teacher in the classroom. Ask yourself this...do you truly know the difference? It's okay if the answer is "no," and it's okay if the answer is "yes" too. Either way, we're about to break it down.

**First and foremost:** the students? They are **not** your children. They are your students. That distinction matters more than most people realize. Yes, you can care deeply for them. Yes, you can love them with all your heart. I know I've stayed up late at night worrying about my own students.

There have been times I've cried over their pain. I have also celebrated their wins like a proud uncle or big brother. But love doesn't give you the license to blur the lines. At the end of the day, you are not their parent. Your job isn't to raise them. Your job is to teach them. To guide, not govern. To support, not smother. To lead, not control. That means you can't bring your home rules into your classroom like they're the Gospel according to you. You cannot (although many do) enforce your household expectations in a space that belongs to them. The classroom is a shared space. A professional space. A learning space.

*You have to know your place, or you'll overstep it. And once you do that...trust gets shaky.*

Students start pulling back. They stop sharing. They stop showing up as their full selves. Why? Because they no longer feel safe, not physically, but emotionally. They feel judged. Controlled. Preached at instead of being taught. When we confuse our role, we shift from educators to enforcers. That's not who we were called to be. (see chapters 3&4). They already have parents. What they need is you. They need a steady, compassionate adult who can hold space without trying to own it. Someone who understands that love in the classroom is powerful, but it needs boundaries to be effective. You can love them, but you must still lead them. And to lead them...well, you must never forget your role.

I say this with love and from experience. Sometimes as educators, we let the power of the position get to our heads. We walk into that classroom thinking respect comes automatically because we are the adults. After all, we have the degrees and we have the authority. Well, here's the truth...respect is not automatic. It's not a right that comes with your educator badge. It's something you have to earn every single day.

I've seen teachers demand it. I've seen them raise their voices, slam doors, and call kids out in front of their peers. They expect students to just fall in line because the educators are the ones in charge. But what those educators are building isn't discipline; it's fear. And fear never builds genuine respect. It builds distance. It builds resentment.

I'll be honest...early in my career, I was guilty of this too. I thought the louder I spoke, the more control I had. I thought "challenging me" meant "disrespecting me." So, I shut students down. I made examples out of kids in front of the whole class. I told myself I was teaching them respect and accountability, but deep down, I was protecting my ego.

Then I had a moment that changed me. I heard a story that stayed with me, one I often go back to again and again. A veteran teacher shared it during a staff development session. He talked about a student named Tasha. She was sharp. Always thinking, always asking. Not the kind of student who caused trouble, but the kind who challenged ideas because she cared. She had a voice, and she used it. One day, during a lesson, Tasha raised her hand and asked why they were learning the material in a certain way. Her question wasn't rude. It was honest. But as the teacher, he was caught off guard and irritated. So he interpreted her question as disrespect. He didn't stop to think; he just clapped back at her. He told her to stop being difficult and kicked her out of the classroom.

Later, he found Tasha standing alone in the hallway. She wasn't yelling. She wasn't angry. She just looked disappointed. She said, "I wasn't trying to fight you. I just wanted to understand. You didn't even listen." When the teacher shared the story again during the staff development session, he said that moment shook him. It made him pause and think, not just about how he acted, but why. He realized it wasn't about discipline. It was about ego. It was about control. Her question wasn't a challenge to his authority. It was an invitation to connect, and he missed it.

When I heard that story, it hit me too. Tasha was right. The teacher reacted instead of responding. He took it personally when it wasn't personal at all, and I saw myself in that. I had done the same thing before numerous times, mistaking curiosity for defiance, letting pride get in the way of listening. That day changed something in me. I started paying more attention. I stopped assuming every tough question was a threat. I stopped leading with my title and started leading with connection.

To do any job in education well, you have to know yourself. Know what sets you off. Know your triggers. Know what buttons students might push, intentionally or not...because they will push them, guaranteed. If you haven't figured out how to identify and navigate your triggers, you're going to crash out. And when you lose it, your class feels it. It's like being the captain of a ship in a storm, if you panic, the crew does too. Even if you're headed straight into chaos, they'll follow your lead.

That's why boundaries are key. But not just boundaries for students, I'm talking about boundaries for you. What are you willing to take home? What are you not? What energy do you let live in your head after the bell rings? If you don't define those lines, you'll crash out every time, and you will burn out. You'll carry every tough conversation, every bad day, every moment of disrespect like a weight on your back and shoulders.

So, set the tone early. Know your limits. Know when to walk away. Know when to tap out. Know when to pause and breathe instead of reacting. That's not weakness, that's wisdom.

This work isn't about dominance and control. Forget about control. It's about influence. And real influence only happens when there is trust. Respect is the foundation, and you can't demand what you haven't earned.

There's another story that comes to mind, one shared by a teacher reflecting on the early years of his career. It was during his second year in the classroom that he had a student whom we will call Malik. Malik had a brilliant mind, a sharp tongue, and he was a natural challenger.

Malik questioned everything, pushed back on directions, and never let an idea slide by without testing it. At first, the teacher took it personally. He saw Malik's constant questioning as defiance, as disrespect. But over time, something clicked. He began to realize that his reactions weren't really about Malik, they were about himself. He hadn't left his ego at the door. He wasn't responding as an educator; he was reacting like someone trying to prove a point. Trying to parent, not teach.

But once that teacher made that internal shift, once he stopped trying to dominate and started trying to understand, everything changed. He began to really listen. He was able to hear what Malik was trying to say beneath the sharp tone. And what he found wasn't a disrespectful kid; it was a student who wanted to be seen. A student who needed engagement, not correction. Malik was a student who pressure-tested things as a way of vetting them.

In the end, Malik didn't need discipline; he needed recognition. And it took a teacher stepping back from himself to truly give that. This brings me to share something for you to ponder as educators: styles make fights. That is a saying used in boxing, but it is relevant in education as well. You have got to know your style, your approach.

What's your rhythm? What is your approach? What are your non-negotiables? What do you truly believe? Because if you walk into that room not knowing who you are, your classroom will find out before you do.

Some of us carry old-school mindsets into today's classroom. Some of us hang on to legacy practices for dear life. While some traditions have value, not all of them translate. "Because I said so" might work at home. It might have worked for you growing up, but in a classroom, with a new generation of thinkers, that just won't cut it. You've got to adapt.

Because not all students are created equally. What worked for Jada won't work for Marcus. What worked for your first-period class may crash and burn in the fourth period.

Teaching isn't about one-size-fits-all. It's about flexibility. It's about meeting kids where they are. Which means... we, the adults, need to adjust. Not the kid. If a student didn't learn it, chances are, we didn't teach it the way they needed. That's not a failure on their part. That's a wake-up call for us.

Have you ever tried teaching a kid the same way over and over, and wondered why it's just not clicking? That's like trying to open every lock with the same key. Doesn't matter how hard you jiggle it...it won't fit. It won't turn. Some students need a different key. A different rhythm. A different kind of reach.

Sometimes you've got to pause. Step back. Look at what's really going on. Sometimes you've got to change the plan mid-lesson, mid-sentence, mid-thought, and just talk to the student.

Hear them out. See them. And that's not a weakness. That's teaching.

There was a student named Devin. He was smart, but always on edge. Never sat still. He would shut down the moment something felt off. For weeks, his teacher tried the usual playbook; notes home, structured seating, extra help after school. None of it worked. One day, the teacher dropped the lesson altogether and just asked him how he was doing. Turns out his mom had been in and out of the hospital, and he was scared, trying to hold it together. That conversation between the teacher and Devin did more than any worksheet ever could. From that day on, Devin started showing up...not just in class, but to class. Sometimes, they don't need a lesson plan. They need a lifeline.

Now, don't get it twisted. I'm not saying let kids run wild. Structure matters. Boundaries matter. Classrooms need order, not chaos. But there's a difference between guiding and controlling. Our job isn't to make students into mini versions of us. It's to help them become the best version of themselves that they can be. That means knowing when to step in and when to step back. Knowing when to speak and when to lead by example.

Not every lesson needs to come from a speech. Some lessons are learned in how we carry ourselves. In how we handle stress. In how we treat people who challenge us. Students are always watching, even when we think they're not listening.

**So let me leave you with this:**

- Know your limit. Know your role. Know your balance.
- You're not their parent. You're their teacher.
- You cannot control everything, and you should not carry everything. Focus on your Circle of Influence.

If you do it right, that's more than enough. Because teaching, real teaching, is not just about the subject. It's about the connection. And that connection is where the power lies.

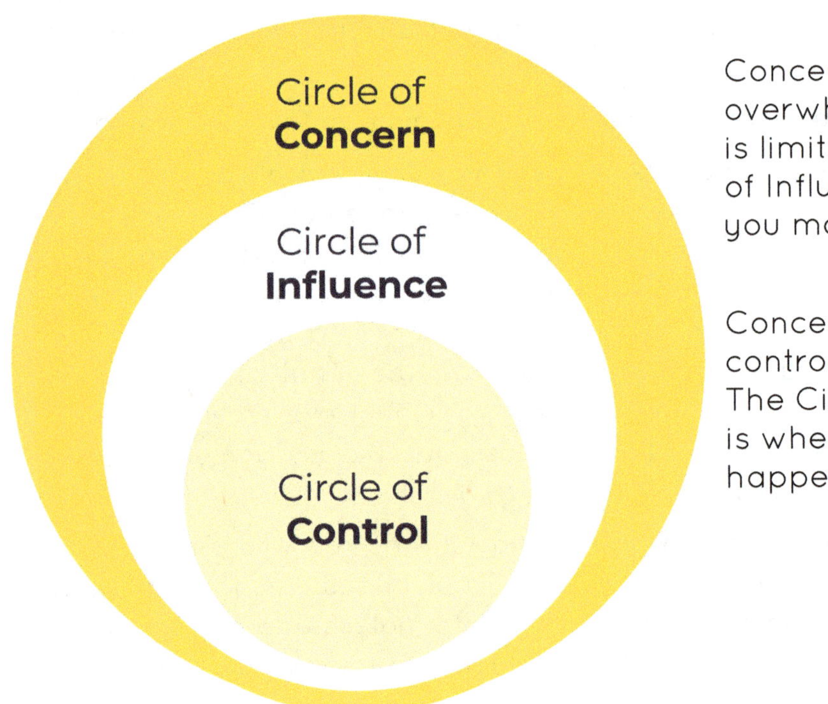


Concern is overwhelming, control is limiting. The Circle of Influence is where you make a difference.

Concern is too broad, control is too limited. The Circle of Influence is where real impact happens.

*DIFFERENT ROLES, SHARED PURPOSE; CARE THAT RESPECTS BOUNDARIES IS THE SWEET SPOT.*

CHAPTER 10

# RECOGNIZE A POWER STRUGGLE DON'T TAKE THE BAIT

No matter who you are or what you do, every one of us has struggled with something. If not now, then in the past. And if not at all, it's probably just around the corner. Struggles are part of life. Struggles assess our growth. Struggles test our patience, challenge our pride, and, especially in this field, pull at our control. Power struggles in the classroom? Oh, those are real. However, the trap we fall into as educators is thinking that we have to win every time, or even properly defining what 'winning' means. We have to prove our authority in the moment. That if we don't shut it down right now, we'll lose. But the truth is...sometimes "winning" in the moment just means losing trust in the long run.

When you notice a power struggle rising with a student, that's not the time to stick out your chest or stand taller. That's the time to check yourself. Because how you handle that moment will either lead to growth or damage. And the real power? It's in knowing the difference.

## WHY ARE YOU ARGUING WITH KIDS?

Let's pause and ask the real question here: "Why are you arguing with a child?"

Seriously. Why are you letting a teenager or pre-teen pull you into a verbal tug-of-war? Why are you letting a fourteen-year-old dictate your mood for the rest of the day?

Every time you argue with a student, you are doing more than stepping out of your role; you're handing your power over one piece at a time. And the worst part? You might not even realize it.

You might think you're proving a point. That your tone, your sharp comeback, or your raised voice is making you look strong and in control. But what you're really doing is showing you're not fully in control of yourself.

Students can see it. Even the ones who say they don't care are watching you more closely than you know, often as entertainment. They're reading your body language, clocking the tone in your voice, checking your facial expression. They see when you're irritated, when you're flustered, when you're two seconds away from going off and crashing out. Some of them are waiting for that moment.

But not because they hate you. Not always because they're trying to be disrespectful. Sometimes it's because they're angry at someone else. Or they're embarrassed and don't know how to handle it. Or they feel powerless in other parts of their life. Perhaps it's at home, with peers, or even just inside their own head. And you, standing in front of them with rules, authority, and expectations, become the outlet for all that tension.

One middle school teacher fell into this trap with a student named Dante. Every day, Dante would come into class with a chip on his shoulder. He'd mumble under his breath, refuse to participate, and challenge everything the teacher said.

One day, after being told to take out his notebook, Dante snapped back, "Why don't you take out yours and do some real teaching?" The teacher, already frustrated from an earlier incident, fired back, "Why don't you take your attitude and go see the principal?" Dante responded, "I hate this class," to the teacher's response of, "This class hates you too."

Now, on the surface, that seems like a fair exchange. But what really happened was this: a wounded student lashed out, and a wounded adult met him in that place of pain. And instead of diffusing the moment, it escalated.

What if the teacher had paused? Took a breath? Said something like, "I hear that you're frustrated, but I'm not here to argue with you. I'm here to help you. If you're not ready to learn right now, I'll give you a minute, but we're not doing this."

That response would not have weakened the teacher. It would have made him wiser. More in control. More respected. Why?

Control doesn't come from volume. Power doesn't come from dominance. Respect doesn't come from who yells louder or has the snappiest comeback.

It comes from consistency. From emotional stability. From how well you manage yourself when the situation gets hard. There is a transfer of energy when a student is projecting negative energy, as you respond with the same energy. The student is actually in control and now has control of their stability, and trading it out for instability.

Mr. Warner was teaching his History class. Two students, Reggie and Tarrence, were talking and being disruptive. After being redirected to quiet down and pay attention, Reggie responded, "SMD," (IYKYK). This was definitely behavior that warranted a consequence. But the response was masterful. It was a masterclass in not taking the bait. Mr. Warner could have been triggered by the invitation to Reggie's private parts, but his classic response was, "No, Thank You." The class erupted in laughter!

Another teacher I know, Ms. Jackson, once said something that I feel holds a lot of weight. She said, "When a kid throws you a rope to pull you into a power struggle, don't pick it up. Let them hold the rope alone, until they realize you're not playing tug-of-war."

Students do hold power. They hold power in how they show up, how they respond, and how they use their voice. And we should never try to strip them of that. Our power as adults is different. We hold the power of response. That's our strength. That's our lane. Too often, we trade that power for ego. For pride. For the need to feel and be "right."

So, the next time a student tests you, challenges you, or throws a verbal jab, don't take the bait. That's not your fight. Your role is bigger than that. Your influence runs deeper than a comeback line. You are the thermostat, not the thermometer. You set the tone.

When you choose to respond with calm insead of heat, you're not just keeping your power, you're teaching them how to find theirs without hurting others.

That's the kind of classroom leadership that lasts.

*YOU DON'T WIN POWER STRUGGLES BY FIGHTING THEM. YOU WIN BY CHOOSING NOT TO ENGAGE.*

## RESPOND, DON'T REACT

The key is this: respond...don't react.

There's a world of difference between the two. Reactions are quick. Emotional. They come from a place of being triggered when we feel challenged, disrespected, or out of control. Reactions are often about us, not the student. Responses, on the other hand, come from a place of clarity and purpose. They're thoughtful. Measured. Intentional. And most of all, they're grounded in the understanding that we are the adults in the room.

There was a high school teacher, Ms. Grant, who once shared a story during a PD (professional development) session. She had a student named Keon who had a reputation for being disruptive. One day, while she was introducing a new lesson, Keon blurted out, "This is dumb! Ain't nobody tryna learn this mess."

She could feel herself tense up. Her pride kicked in. Part of her wanted to shut him down hard and fast, to remind him who was in charge. But instead, she paused. She took a slow breath, and then she said, "Keon, I hear that you're frustrated. You don't have to like what I'm teaching, but you do have to respect the space we're in. Can we talk about this after class?"

Keon didn't respond right away, but he didn't say another word for the rest of the period. Later that day, he came by her room and said, "You didn't embarrass me. You could've, but you didn't. That was cool."

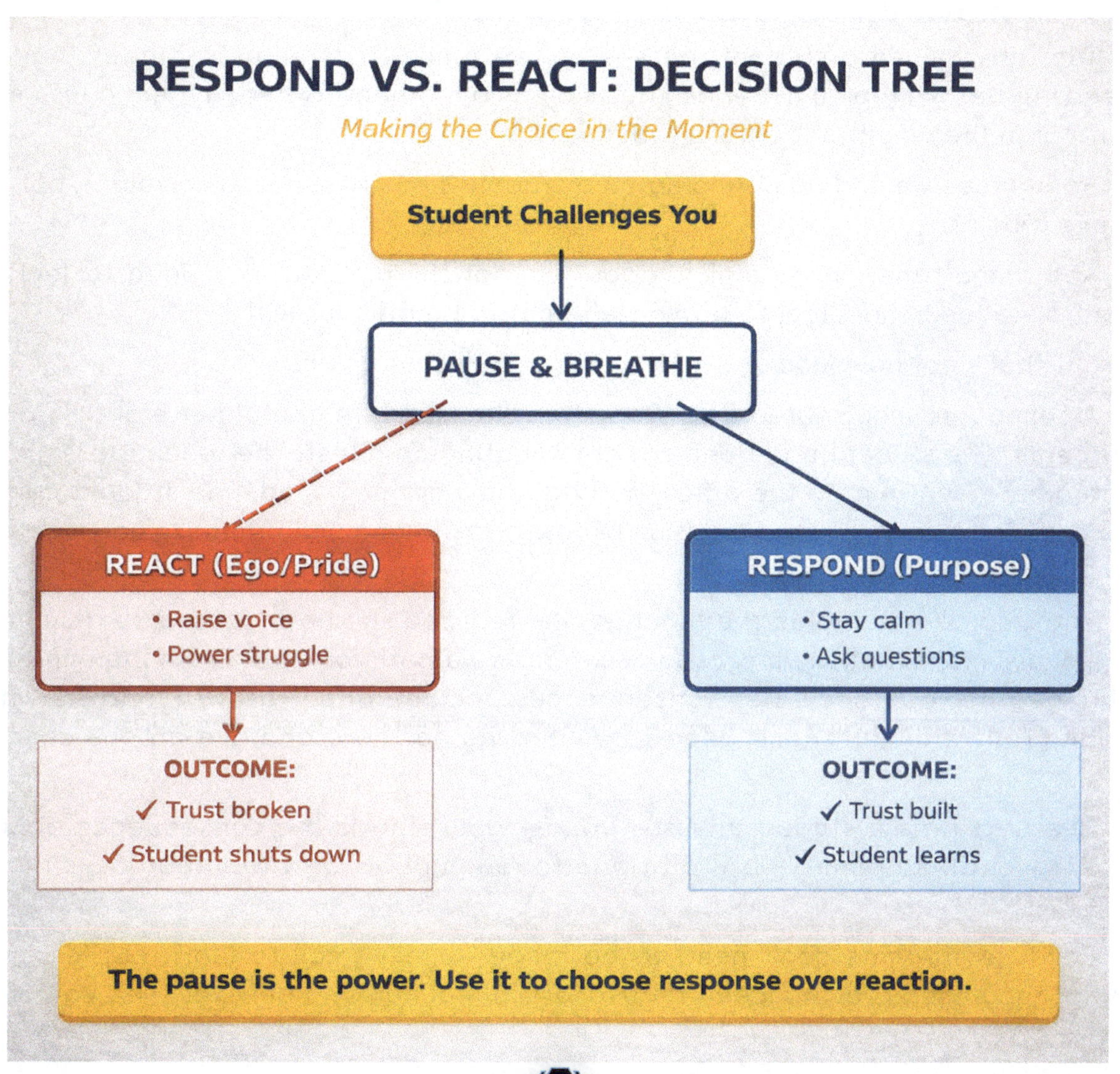

And just like that, a door opened.

It would've been easy for Ms. Grant to match Keon's energy, to react. But she didn't. She responded with calm and care, and that choice earned her something far more powerful than control: it earned her trust.

## DON'T POUND ON THE MISTAKE | BUILD FROM IT

Too often, when a student messes up, we make that moment bigger than it needs to be. We replay it. Rehash it. Use it as a moment to "teach them a lesson", but not in the way that actually teaches.

Sometimes we end up pounding on a student's mistake, not to correct it, but to make a point.

And many times that point is about us, not them. About our need to feel in control, to feel respected, to prove we're not to be messed with.

But that's not how kids grow. That's how they shut down.

A colleague once shared a conversation she had with one of her eighth-grade students. The student had been caught cheating on a test. The teacher assigned him a zero, sent him to the office, and had his parents called. The student came back the next day and said quietly, "I know I was wrong. But it felt like you wanted to hurt me, not help me fix it."

That moment humbled the teacher. She realized she had focused so much on the punishment that she forgot to help him see a path forward. From then on, she changed her approach. Her consequences became about growth, retakes with added reflection questions, peer accountability partners, and one-on-one check-ins.

The next time a student messes up, ask yourself: "Is the consequence about growth, or about control? Is it a bridge to redemption, or a wall that locks them out?"

Because students don't need to be made to feel small to learn big lessons. What they need is a chance to rebuild, and a teacher who believes they can.

## KNOW YOUR POWER | AND KNOW WHEN TO STEP ASIDE

There's a quiet confidence in knowing your power, and an even deeper wisdom in knowing when to step aside.

Teaching isn't about being in control every second. It's about helping students learn to control themselves. It's about modeling composure, compassion, and consistency.

Think about the role of a coach. A coach doesn't run onto the field every time the game gets intense. They don't fight every battle for their players. But they prepare their team. They guide from the sideline. And when the moment gets heated, a good coach doesn't panic. Rather, they focus. The same goes for teaching.

Ms. Ortega, a veteran teacher in an alternative school, had a student named Jason who constantly challenged her. He pushed limits, tested boundaries, and made almost every instruction a negotiation. But Ms. Ortega never fought with him. Instead, she would say, "Jason, I see you trying to have the last word. I'm not interested in that. I'm interested in who you're becoming."

She knew when to hold the line, and when to give space. And over time, Jason's behavior shifted. Not because she out-argued him, but because she out-loved him.

She never tried to dominate; she aimed to develop.

Stepping back doesn't mean giving up control. It means choosing influence over intimidation. When students realize you're not trying to defeat them, but trying to defend their future, that's when the real shift happens.

## FINAL THOUGHTS: GRACE OVER PRIDE

There's power in stillness. There's strength in grace.

In a classroom full of voices, moods, hormones, and noise, the one who stays calm, who doesn't flinch when challenged, is the one who leads.

Grace is not weakness. It's wisdom. It's knowing that just because you can shut a student down, it doesn't mean you should. Just because you can punish, doesn't mean it will help. Just because you feel disrespected doesn't mean you have to become disrespectful.

You don't win arguments with students. You win their trust when you show them that your love, your leadership, and your belief in them aren't conditional on their worst moment.

So, next time a student steps out of line or pushes your buttons, take a breath. Ask yourself: Is this about my pride or their growth?

You're not in that classroom to prove how powerful you are. You're there to show them how powerful they can become when someone believes in them, even when they're hard to believe in.

And sometimes, the strongest move you can make is not to raise your voice, but to raise the bar with love.

Stay calm. Stay kind. Stay rooted in purpose. Because that's where the real power lives.

CHAPTER 11

# ACCEPT FEEDBACK
# YOUR STUDENTS ARE TALKING

*FEEDBACK ISN'T AN ATTACK. IT'S A GIFT. OPEN IT.*

You've earned the degree; maybe even more than one. You've studied the theory, completed the coursework, and endured the long nights of planning and preparation. Now you stand in front of students with the title: teacher. That title carries weight. It carries responsibility. And it's easy, after all that effort, to feel like you've arrived. Like you're supposed to have the answers.

But here's the truth...*none of us knows it all.*

That's not a weakness. It's a reality of the work we do. Teaching isn't a destination; it's a lifelong process of learning, unlearning, and growing. The moment we believe we've mastered it all is the moment we stop being effective. Every year, every class, every student, every day brings something new. And if we are not open to learning, especially from the very students we serve, we miss the chance to become the educators our students truly need.

## FEEDBACK IS NOT AN ATTACK | IT'S A GIFT

It never ceases to amaze me how so many adults walk around all day giving adjusting feedback to children, most times unsolicited feedback, expecting them to take it, accept it, and even thank them for it. The same adults have the thinnest skin known to man. They make no space to receive any feedback. Some of us treat feedback like it's an insult; like someone questioning our methods means we're being disrespected. But feedback doesn't mean you're failing. It means there is room to grow...and that's a good thing. It means someone sees your *potential.*

Let's shift perspectives for a moment. Think about the most successful companies in the world. I'm talking about the ones that lead their industries and build loyal communities around their brands. *What do they all have in common?* They prioritize feedback. They don't just launch a product and assume it's perfect. They ask questions. They gather input. They study patterns in what people love, what frustrates them, and what's missing. Most importantly, they listen. They adapt. That's how they grow.

Now, the companies that refuse to listen; the ones that double down on being "right" even when the evidence says otherwise; they fade. Their audience shrinks, because ignoring the people you serve is the fastest way to lose them.

Now bring that same lens to the classroom. You may not sell a product, but you *do* provide a daily experience of you, and your students are the ones living that experience in real time. They know what's working. They feel what's not. They see the moments when the lesson connects, and the moments when it doesn't land at all.

Take this story shared during a professional development session. A veteran teacher described a quiet student in her class. This is a girl who rarely spoke up, kept her head down, and struggled to pass. The teacher had assumed the student simply wasn't trying, but during a student feedback circle, that young girl finally spoke up.

She said, *"You move on too fast. I get lost and then I give up."*

That one sentence shifted everything. The teacher believed she was being efficient and that she was keeping the class moving to cover the material. But to that student, the pace felt like a sprint she couldn't keep up with. She wasn't just disengaged. She was overwhelmed, which led to disengagement.

After hearing that, the teacher made intentional changes. She slowed down her lessons, built in checkpoints to see who was really following along, and gave students more time to process and respond to the material being presented. The difference was immediate. That same student began turning in stronger work. Her confidence grew. Beyond that, the teacher gained a deeper understanding of how her students were experiencing her classroom. This was not based on assumptions but based on honest feedback.

If you don't listen to your students, their words, their behavior, even their silence, how can you truly say you're doing your best work? There is absolutely no way you can respond adequately. Feedback is the bridge between good intentions and real impact. Our students are always offering something. The question is: are we paying attention?

## THE CLASSROOM RUNS ON STUDENT VOICE

**Ask yourself this:** *Do your students truly believe their voices matter in your classroom? Or do they feel like passengers on a train they didn't board by choice? Are they strapped in while someone else chooses the direction, speed, and destination, with no option to speak up or slow down?*

Too often, students feel like school happens to them, not with them. They're expected to follow, not question. Obey, not contribute. And when that's the dynamic, real learning, the kind rooted in curiosity, trust, and critical thinking can't fully take root.

Giving students a voice in your classroom doesn't mean you give up authority. It means you choose to share power with purpose. You show them that leadership isn't about control, it's about connection. When students realize that their voices don't just echo into silence but actually shape the learning environment... something powerful happens. They lean in. They participate. They start to take ownership, not just of their grades, but of the community you're building together.

That kind of trust doesn't appear just because you say, "I care what you think." Students have been told that before, from adults who didn't mean it. You have to earn their belief in your sincerity.

That work starts with authenticity. Earlier in this book, we talked about what it means to show up as your real self. That includes flaws, questions, and all. We also explored the concept of productive strain and the healthy tension that comes from letting students make real choices and take real risks. Those same foundations (authenticity and agency) are the conditions that allow honest feedback to grow.

Students need to see that your classroom is a living space, an ecosystem, not a script. That it evolves, that it listens, and that it values them not just as learners, but as thinkers, truth-tellers, and collaborators. When they see that, their feedback won't just be more honest...it'll be more insightful, more constructive, and more courageous.

When students believe their voices matter, they use their voices, and that's when the real work begins.

When you've done that work, you can ask real questions:

- "What's helping you learn in here?"
- "What's getting in your way?"
- "What do I do that makes this class better or worse for you?"

Then you listen; and really hear them.

## STUDENTS GIVE FEEDBACK ALL THE TIME | ARE YOU PAYING ATTENTION?

**Here's the thing:** Even if you never ask for feedback, your students are giving it to you. *Every. Single. Day.* It shows up in the silence. It shows up when they shut down. It shows up when they challenge your rules. It shows up when they don't turn in work, or when they flat out refuse to do it.

That's feedback.

- *A student who won't speak in class? Maybe they don't feel safe.*
- *A student who won't work with certain classmates? That might be about race, gender, or past trauma.*
- *A student who questions your expectations? They might not trust your fairness, or they might not believe you believe in them.*

We have to be honest. Sometimes we create classrooms where students feel judged, not supported. Sometimes we carry pride, ego, or even unconscious bias into our spaces. Feedback helps us confront that.

And...yes, it hurts sometimes. Nobody wants to hear they made a kid feel small. But if that's happening, wouldn't you want to know?

## YOU CAN LEARN FROM YOUR STUDENTS | IF YOU'RE WILLING

Some of the best lessons I have ever learned did not come from a professional development workshop. They came from my students.

There's something powerful about the stories educators share behind closed doors. They are the stories that never make it into lesson plans or staff meetings but stay with them for years. They're the moments that shift how a teacher sees the classroom and themselves.

One educator shared the story of a student who pulled her aside after class and said, *"You always assume we're not trying when we ask for help. That makes me not want to ask anymore."* The teacher had no idea her tone was shutting down the very effort she was trying to encourage. She'd thought she was holding students accountable. But in that moment, she realized her assumptions were cutting off trust, assuming the worst vs. the best. This is deficit-based thinking that we engage in, often unconsciously. Naming it creates the opportunity for disruption. From that day on, she started approaching student struggles with curiosity instead of judgment. She approached students by asking more questions, listening more deeply, and seeing effort where she had once seen defiance.

In another episode of ***"Have You Ever Heard That Before,"*** a teacher recalled a moment during her student reflection circle, where a student quietly said, *"You always call on the same three kids."* Then continued with, *"other people can answer."* It wasn't said with anger, just honesty. And that "honesty" stung. The teacher hadn't noticed the pattern, but once it was named, she couldn't unsee it. She began tracking participation, mixing up how she facilitated discussions, and making sure every student had space to contribute, not just the more confident or outspoken ones. These kinds of truths are never easy to hear. They challenge our instincts. They expose blind spots, and they're necessary.

What's clear across all these stories is this. Students will teach you about yourself if you are willing to listen, reflect, and learn. They'll reveal the quiet consequences of our routines. They'll shine light on the small things we overlook that end up mattering most. They'll remind us that good intentions aren't enough. Impact is what counts.

The most transformational growth doesn't always come from books, training, or observation checklists. Sometimes, it comes from the brave honesty of a student who tells the truth, even when it's hard to hear. And in those moments, we are given the chance to become more than just better educators. We are given the chance to become better human beings.

## YOU CAN'T GROW IF YOU DON'T LISTEN

**So, here's the final question:** *Are you willing to take feedback from your students because they are your students? Or are you unwilling to take feedback because they are your students?*

The answer to that question says a lot about the kind of educator you are, and the kind you are becoming.

Look, this work is not about being perfect. It's about being real. It's about showing your students that you don't have to know everything to be worth listening to. We all hold a piece of the truth. You just have to be open. Honest. Humble. And willing to grow.

The truth is, your students are always communicating something.

***The real question is: Are you listening?***

CHAPTER 12

# CHANGE THE GAME | BE THE SHIFT

***"EVERYONE WANTS TO FIND THE RIGHT PERSON, BUT FEW ARE WILLING TO BECOME THE RIGHT PERSON."***

*CHANGE THE GAME BY BECOMING THE CHANGE.*

Often used in the context of relationships, this quote speaks volumes about education as well. In classrooms across the country, many teachers are hoping to be assigned "the right kind of student." You know the ones who come in motivated, respectful, eager to learn, and easy to manage. But far too often, we fail to flip that lens inward. The real question is: Are we being the kind of teachers our students need at this moment?

It's easy to fall into the rhythm of routine...especially if it once worked. But the truth is, the game has changed.

Society is shifting. The world outside our school walls is faster, louder, and more complex, and students are evolving right along with it. They communicate differently, process differently, and respond to different cues than students did even a decade ago. And yet, too many classrooms are still being run on outdated models that no longer fit the students sitting in them.

One veteran teacher, Mr. Daniels, spent over twenty years teaching social studies with high expectations and a traditional structure. His lessons were clear, his lectures well-prepared, and his discipline consistent. But over time, he started noticing that students weren't engaging the same way they used to. They were distracted, unmotivated, and disconnected. For a while, he chalked it up to "kids these days." But eventually, he sat down and asked himself a hard question: Am I really reaching them, or just going through motions that feel familiar to me?

Then there was Ms. Rivas, an elementary teacher known for her creativity. Even with her passion, she hit a wall when her usual classroom strategies stopped working. Instead of doubling down, she observed how students interacted with each other, what held their attention, and where they showed natural curiosity. She started shifting her lessons to include more collaboration, digital tools, and real-world connections. Within weeks, student behavior improved, not because she added new rules, but because she changed her approach.

These are not stories of failure. They are stories of reflection and courageous adaptation. Because the reality is: the methods that brought success in the past may not move today's learners forward.

If you're still relying on the same worksheets, the same seating charts, the same reward systems that worked five, ten, or fifteen years ago...if your lesson plans haven't grown with your students...then the gap between teaching and learning will only widen. You can't expect different results from the same worn-out strategies.

Change doesn't happen by accident. It's intentional. It's uncomfortable. But most of all, it's necessary.

You must change to see change.

## STYLE VS. SUBSTANCE

Every educator enters the classroom with their own unique rhythm. Some lean into structure and routine, others bring humor and spontaneity. Some teachers build their space around calm consistency; others thrive in the energy of flexible, hands-on learning. There is no single correct style. What matters is that your style supports student access and success.

But while style can shape the classroom environment, it is substance that truly drives learning.

At the heart of our work are two critical questions:

- Are you truly teaching your students?
- And more importantly, are your students actually learning?

Those two questions are not interchangeable. They speak to the difference between instruction and impact. You can deliver content, assign tasks, and follow your pacing guide to the letter...and still have students who are disengaged, confused, or quietly falling behind. Teaching is not measured by how much ground you cover, but by how much your students carry with them once they leave your room.

One middle school teacher, Mr. Henson, was well-liked and known for his relaxed classroom atmosphere. He prided himself on being approachable and giving students plenty of space to express themselves. But when his test scores came back low, and student feedback pointed to unclear expectations, he took a hard look at his approach. He realized that while his students felt comfortable, they weren't being consistently challenged. His teaching style was there, but the substance wasn't always landing.

On the other end of the spectrum, Ms. Cho ran a tight, structured classroom. Every minute of instruction was planned, and her lessons were rigorous. Yet over time, she noticed more students becoming emotionally withdrawn. Assignments were turned in, but students weren't engaging in discussions or taking intellectual risks. In her case, the substance was present, but the delivery lacked the human connection students needed to stay engaged.

The most effective educators are the ones who can strike a delicate balance between style and substance. The ones who know when to adjust, when to stretch, and when to step back and listen. They are not driven by a need to be seen as "the best." They are driven by a deep responsibility to do their best to reflect, to grow, and to show up better each day than the day before.

That's where real change begins.

## RESPECT ISN'T GIVEN. NEITHER IS TRUST

Stepping into a classroom doesn't automatically come with trust. It doesn't matter how long you've been teaching, how many degrees you've earned, or how many conferences you've presented at. You could have thirty years of experience and still walk into a room full of students who don't know you and who are not ready to follow you until you show them why they should.

Experience might open the door, but character is what keeps it open.

In too many schools, trust is treated like a teacher entitlement, something owed rather than earned. But students don't operate on that assumption. They assess your energy before your credentials. They respond to consistency, not titles. They are watching to see if your words match your actions, if your reactions stay fair, and if your presence is real.

A high schooler once said about her favorite teacher, "He never let us slide, but we always knew he had our back." That teacher, Mr. Clay, didn't get trust because he was the funniest or most lenient; he got trust because he was reliable. He followed through. He didn't belittle his students when they made mistakes. And he didn't talk down to them just because he held the authority in the room.

Then there's the opposite story, teachers who expect students to respect them simply because of their age, their title, or their tenure. Ms. Price, a long-serving educator in an urban district, struggled to connect with her incoming ninth-graders. Her methods hadn't changed in years, and her tone often came across as dismissive. Students kept their distance. Assignments weren't completed. Behavior issues escalated. It wasn't until she started attending student-led events and asking for their feedback on classroom routines that her relationships began to change. Slowly, trust began to build, but only after she acknowledged that it had to be earned.

Trust is not about being "cool" or trying to win students over. It's about being consistent, present, and authentic. Students don't need perfection, but they do need to know that you see them, hear them, and care about them as people, not just as names on a roster.

If they believe in your presence, they will begin to believe in your purpose. But if they can't trust you, they won't learn from you. Period.

## YOU DON'T ADJUST ONCE | YOU ADJUST CONSTANTLY

Adaptation in education is not a single event; it's a way of thinking, a continuous process that requires awareness, humility, and the courage to evolve. The ability to shift, pivot, and respond to the needs of students is not a luxury in today's classroom...it's a necessity.

When some educators hear the word change, there's often resistance. Change in any form, curriculum, priorities, or change management in general, unearths so many fears. For many, it brings the fear of losing what they've worked so hard to build. But true change does not erase your teaching identity. It refines it. It doesn't erase your foundation. It strengthens it.

Adjustment is not about abandoning what's familiar. It's about expanding your perspective and fine-tuning your practice. Just as we provide accommodations and modifications for students with unique learning needs, we, too, must be willing to modify ourselves and our strategies, our delivery, our mindset.

Take Ms. Wallace, for example. She had spent years developing a set of lessons that were both rigorous and aligned to standards. But when she transitioned to a new city in a different part of the network, her classroom began shifting culturally, more students coming from different linguistic backgrounds and varying social-emotional needs, a bit more unfamiliar, her usual materials began falling flat. Instead of blaming student motivation or questioning their readiness, she took a step back and asked herself, What needs to shift in me to meet them where they are? What do I need to learn to add to my tool belt? She began to read some recommended books. She revised her lessons to include more visuals, collaborative learning, and real-world relevance. The outcome? Not only did her students' engagement rise, but so did their performance.

The most grounded educators are the ones who stay curious, not just about their subject, but about their students. They don't cling to the way things used to be. They examine why things are the way they are now, and how they can prepare students for the world ahead using both experience and adaptability.

And here's a truth we often overlook: the message you intend to send is not always the message students receive. Just because you speak with clarity or passion doesn't mean the student hears what you hoped they would. This disconnect isn't always about the words...it's about tone, timing, trust, and emotional context. That's why reflection and revision are not optional...they are essential.

Teaching is not just about delivering content. It is about being aware of how that content lands. And when it doesn't land right, it's on us not to give up, but to adjust.

## A SHIFT IN PRACTICE: THE STORY OF MR. LEWIS

In every school, some educators begin their careers believing that control is the key to classroom success. Mr. Lewis was one of them. A structured and disciplined teacher, he took pride in his organized environment. His rules were clear, his tone firm, and his expectations non-negotiable. Desks were always in perfect rows. Voices were low. Assignments were submitted on time. On paper, his classroom was in order.

But something essential was missing.

His students followed directions, but they didn't lean in. They complied, but they didn't connect. Learning was happening, but trust wasn't. For years, Mr. Lewis believed that keeping a tight grip on the classroom was the only way to ensure academic progress until one particular class challenged that belief.

That year, he was assigned a group of students who did not respond to his usual methods. Jamari, a bright but quiet student, began shutting down during lessons. Every time his voice rose, his eyes lowered. Destiny, a once-consistent student, started skipping class altogether. Others began withdrawing emotionally or acting out in subtle ways. Mr. Lewis could have pointed fingers and blamed the students, their home lives, or the "new generation." Instead, he did something far more powerful: she paused. He reflected. And then, he chose to grow.

He began by listening more and speaking less. He shifted from controlling his students to connecting with them. He introduced restorative circles on Fridays to create space for student voices. He asked questions, not just about academics, but about their lives, their interests, their dreams. Slowly, his classroom shifted from a space of compliance to a community of mutual respect and engagement.

By the end of the year, things looked different. The desks were no longer perfectly aligned, but the energy in the room was stronger than ever. Students who had once been guarded began contributing freely. Discipline issues dropped. Academic growth increased. But more importantly, his students felt seen, heard, and valued.

Mr. Lewis didn't lose control; he gained credibility. He didn't let go of expectations; he elevated them. He didn't change the students; he changed himself.

And in doing so, he changed everything.

## CLOSING MESSAGE: BE THE SHIFT

Educators often enter this profession hoping to make a difference. But the truth is, making a difference requires something more than passion or intention. It requires transformation. Not just in students, but in us.

If we want to change the outcomes for our students, we must be willing to change the inputs, our approach, our mindset, our willingness to grow. That means letting go of practices that no longer serve our classrooms. It means refusing to get so comfortable in what's familiar that we lose sight of what's effective. Growth is not a threat to our identity as educators; it is proof that we care enough to evolve.

You don't have to be perfect. But you do have to be present. You don't have to have all the answers. But you do have to ask better questions. You don't have to reinvent who you are. But you do have to reflect on who your students need you to be right now.

Take Mr. Greene, a seasoned teacher who once believed that showing vulnerability was a weakness. After attending a student-led town hall about race, identity, and mental health, he shared a personal story about his own struggles with anxiety. That simple act shifted how his students viewed him. They saw him not just as a teacher, but as a person. The trust that followed transformed his classroom culture, and student engagement skyrocketed.

Or consider Ms. Medina, who was on the verge of leaving the profession after feeling burnt out. Instead of walking away, she began redesigning her curriculum to reflect her students' lived experiences. Literature circles became spaces for critical dialogue. Writing assignments turned into personal narratives. Her students showed up not just with their pencils, but with their full selves. She didn't change careers; she changed her approach. And that saved her work.

## CHANGE THE GAME, AND YOU CHANGE LIVES

Be consistent in your values. Be courageous in your reflection. Be honest about what needs to shift, and bold enough to make it happen.

This work will stretch you. It will test you. But if you lean into the shift, it will also transform you. And in the process, it will open doors for your students that may have once felt locked.

**So, I'll leave you with this: *Are you ready to make the changes that change the game? Or are you still hoping the game will change without you?***

CHAPTER 13

# CONSISTENTLY INCONSISTENT
# MASTER THE PIVOT

***"CONSISTENCY DOESN'T MEAN BEING ROBOTIC. IT MEANS BEING ROOTED. IT MEANS SHOWING UP WITH INTENTION, EVEN WHEN EVERYTHING ELSE AROUND YOU IS SHIFTING."***

## CONSISTENTLY INCONSISTENT

One of the hardest truths to face as educators is this: we are not always consistent. And our students notice.

We may not realize it at the moment, but inconsistency can quietly erode the foundation we are trying to build. It shows up in small ways: saying one thing on Monday and shifting course by Friday. Holding one student to a standard, but letting another slide. Encouraging responsibility while showing up unprepared ourselves. Expecting respect, but offering little patience in return.

And the students? They may not say anything directly, but they are always watching. Always assessing. Always learning from you.

Mr. Thompson, a high school science teacher, was known for his passionate lectures and deep knowledge of content, but his classroom culture was unpredictable. Some days, he was patient; other days, he was quick-tempered. Late work policies changed without warning. Certain students were allowed to joke and play, while others were written up for the same behavior. Over time, his students stopped engaging; not because of the subject, but because they no longer knew what to expect from him. The inconsistency made the space feel unstable, and that instability closed the door to trust.

In contrast, Ms. Patel, an eighth-grade English teacher, made it a priority to be the same teacher every day...even when life got hard. Her students knew her expectations, but they also knew her grace. She greeted them at the door daily, responded to misbehavior with fairness rather than frustration, and followed through on both praise and consequences. Her students knew what she stood for, and that sense of stability created a safe and productive environment for learning.

Being consistent doesn't mean being rigid or perfect. It means being reliable. It means aligning your words with your actions...even on the tough days. It means showing students that your leadership doesn't waver based on mood or moment.

Students don't expect flawlessness, but they do crave something solid to stand on. When they can count on you, they begin to count with you. But when your energy is unpredictable, or your expectations shift based on who's in the room, trust breaks. Once that happens, learning takes a backseat to self-protection.

Consistency is the quiet promise we make to our students every day. Keep it.

## RECOGNIZE THE POWER STRUGGLE

Every educator, no matter how seasoned or new, will eventually encounter a moment in the classroom where their authority is tested, not just by a student's behavior, but by how they choose to respond to it.

It may start with defiance: an eye roll, a refusal to follow directions, or a sharp, offhand comment tossed across the room like a dare. Other times, it's more subtle; a student who withdraws, stops engaging, or quietly challenges your expectations with a look, a sigh, or silence that says more than words.

What you're witnessing in those moments is not always about disrespect. Often, it's about control.

See, students don't enter our classrooms with the same emotional tools we expect them to have. Many are navigating situations that make them feel powerless...at home, in their relationships, in their identity, or simply in how the world treats them. When they step into our classrooms, they sometimes bring that internal chaos with them. And when a young person doesn't know how to name or manage that feeling of being out of control, they do what most people do; they look for something, or someone, to push against.

And if you're not careful, that someone will be you.

That's when the power struggle begins; not because the student wants to "win," but because they want to feel *seen*. They want to feel *heard*. They want to feel *something* other than what's been weighing on them.

And if, in that moment, we take the bait, if we match their energy, if we argue, shout, or punish out of pride rather than purpose, we lose the very authority we think we're defending. We become part of the storm instead of the anchor they need us to be.

Ms. Carter, a committed and passionate middle school teacher in her fifth year, learned this the hard way. There was one student, let's call him Devon, who challenged her nearly every day. His comments were quick, biting, and always timed to get a reaction. And for a while, it worked. Their back-and-forth became a regular performance, one that disrupted the class and left Ms. Carter frustrated and defeated.

She told herself she was "being firm." That she couldn't let him get away with it. But deep down, she knew she was reacting, not leading.

One day, after yet another verbal tug-of-war between Ms. Carter and Devon, a veteran teacher quietly pulled Ms. Carter aside and said, "You keep arguing with him like you're equals. You're not. You're the adult in the room. You have the power, but you're giving it away every time you try to prove it."

That conversation cut deep, but it also opened her eyes. Ms. Carter stopped confronting Devon in front of his peers. She started pulling him aside, speaking to him one-on-one with calmness instead of control. She asked questions instead of giving speeches. And most importantly, she stopped trying to "win."

The shift didn't happen overnight, but it did happen. Over time, Devon's outbursts lessened. The tension started to melt. He saw that she wasn't his enemy, and she saw that his behavior had roots that had nothing to do with her.

As educators, we have to understand something essential: A student's struggle with control isn't always personal, but how we respond to it is. Our classrooms should be places where students learn how to process emotion, not just memorize content. That means we must learn to read between the behaviors. To recognize when a challenge is really a cry for help. To know that our authority is not proven through volume, but through emotional intelligence and restraint.

It's not a weakness to de-escalate. It's not surrender to pause, breathe, and respond with clarity. That's strength. That's strategy. That's real classroom management.

We don't lead through power struggles. *We lead by choosing not to enter them.*

## MASTER RESPONDING VS. REACTING

There's a split-second in every classroom confrontation; a fork in the road where a teacher must decide: *Will I respond...or will I react?*

This choice may seem small in the moment, but it carries weight. Because how we handle those tense, heated exchanges say just as much, if not more, about our leadership than our lesson plans ever could.

Reacting is instinctive. It comes from the gut, fueled by frustration, fatigue, or even fear. It's when words come out too fast and too sharp. It's that sarcastic remark, that elevated tone, that pointed comment made more to sting than to solve.

Responding, on the other hand, is deliberate. It's when we pause to breathe before we speak. It's the calm presence that says, "I'm still in control," not because we're louder, but because we're grounded. Responding means choosing purpose over pride.

Responding doesn't mean letting a student slide. It means addressing the behavior *without* becoming part of it.

And make no mistake...students are watching us. Closely. They're learning how to navigate emotion and authority by watching how we manage ours. For some of them, you may be the first adult who models what it looks like to stand firm without striking back.

Coach Bailey, a veteran high school P.E. teacher, once shared a powerful story. During a heated gym class, one of his students snapped and cursed at him after being benched from a game. The whole gym fell silent, waiting for the blow-up. In previous years, Coach Bailey admitted, he might have sent the student straight to the office for his behavior, zero tolerance, zero conversation.

But this time, he held his ground quietly. He didn't match the student's heat. He simply continued class. Then, after the dust had settled, he pulled the student aside and asked one simple question: "What was that really about?"

The student hesitated, then broke down. It wasn't about basketball. It was about chaos at home. His mother had lost her job, they were about to be evicted, and he felt like everything in his world was slipping through his hands.

That moment changed everything. Not just for the student, but for Coach Bailey. He realized that *responding* opened the door to trust. It gave him access to the student's world; access he would have lost if he had reacted with authority instead of compassion.

Teaching is full of those moments. And each one is a chance to show students what it looks like to manage conflict, to stay rooted in purpose, and to lead with integrity. Every time you respond with intention, you're not just teaching content. You're teaching character.

## THE REAL CONSEQUENCE

Let's be honest...discipline is part of the job. We can't ignore behavior that disrupts learning or disrespects others. But how we *frame* that discipline makes all the difference.

***Real consequences aren't about punishment. They're about purpose.***

Too often, educators mistake consequence for control. We hand out detentions like badges of honor or raise our voices just to remind students who's "in charge."

But let's be clear...that's not discipline. That's ego in a teacher's coat.

The goal of any consequence should be growth, not humiliation. If a student walks away from a consequence feeling embarrassed, resentful, or confused, they didn't learn anything. They just endured something.

But if they walk away with clarity, if they understand why the boundary was set and how to move differently next time, that's when the learning sticks.

Mr. Alvarez, a ninth-grade math teacher, handled a cheating incident in a way that showed just that kind of growth-focused thinking. A student had copied an entire homework assignment from a classmate. When confronted, the student lied, then doubled down.

Instead of launching into a lecture or calling home in anger, Mr. Alvarez sat the student down and said, "I want to understand why you felt like this was your only option. And then I want to help you figure out a better one."

They talked for twenty minutes, not about rules, but about pressure. About the student's fear of failing. About what it means to earn something, even if it's not perfect.

*The consequence*? The student had to redo the assignment and write a short reflection on the importance of honesty in learning.

It wasn't just a penalty; it was a *lesson*.

Accountability should never be about "winning" a power struggle. It should be about guiding students back to the center. That takes patience. It takes humility. And it takes a willingness to move past the surface of a behavior and into its root.

Ask yourself:

- Am I reacting to the student...or responding to the situation?
- Is my consequence teaching something...or just proving something?

A student once said of her teacher, "She never tried to make me feel small when I messed up. She made me feel like I still mattered...even when I was wrong."

That's not soft teaching. That's strong teaching. That's what it means to master the pivot.

## CONSISTENCY ISN'T RIGIDITY

In education, we often preach the value of consistency, and rightly so. Students need to know what to expect from us. They need structure, boundaries, and stability. But let's be clear: consistency does not mean rigidity.

It's not about memorizing scripts or enforcing rules like a machine. True consistency is rooted in *reliability of character*, not uniformity of response.

It means being anchored in your purpose, even as you adjust your approach.

Because the classroom is not a laboratory with controlled variables. It's a living, breathing space filled with unpredictable lives. One student walks in angry because they missed breakfast. Another is anxious from last night's argument at home. A third is carrying trauma no one knows about. So, showing up the same way every single day, without considering context, doesn't make you consistent... it makes you disconnected.

Ms. Rivers, an eighth-grade social studies teacher, once shared a story about a student named Jamal. He had a history of acting out in class; but on this particular day, he was unusually withdrawn. When he refused to participate in a group activity, the usual protocol might've called for a phone call home or a behavior log.

But instead of following the usual routine, Ms. Rivers paused. She pulled Jamal aside and quietly asked, *"Is today a hard day?"* That simple question opened the door. He nodded, fighting back tears. His older brother had been arrested the night before, and Jamal hadn't slept.

That day, her consistency showed up not as discipline, but as compassion. She made space for him to regroup. The next week, Jamal was back on task. He knew she saw him as more than a behavior.

Being "consistently inconsistent" is not a contradiction. It's a commitment to meet students where they are, without abandoning who you are. It's the ability to shift with wisdom, to bend without breaking, and to recognize that equity doesn't always look equal.

It takes strength to do that. Real strength. The kind of strength that isn't loud or forceful, but patient, flexible, and intentional. The kind of strength that keeps showing up...not with a hammer, but with a hand extended.

BEND WITHOUT BREAKING. STAY ROOTED WHILE REACHING.

## FINAL WORD: USE YOUR POWER, DON'T PROVE IT

As educators, we hold tremendous power. The words we say, the way we handle conflict, the energy we bring into a room all matter. But here's the truth: power that needs to be proven is already insecure.

You don't need to raise your voice to raise the standard. You don't need to win an argument to lead a student. Influence isn't about dominating the moment; it's about *directing it* with clarity, calm, and care.

Mr. Glenn, a veteran high school teacher, used to tell new educators, "You don't have to show them who's boss. They already know who's in charge. The question is, 'What will you do with that authority?'"

When a student challenges your boundary, it's tempting to assert control. But the real question isn't, "How do I win this?" The real question is, "How do I lead through this?"

So, the next time you feel that tension rise, the moment when a student tests your patience or pushes your limits, take a breath and ask yourself:

- Am I about to react, or am I choosing to respond?
- Am I leading with pride...or with purpose?
- Am I here to prove my power, or to use it for something greater?

Because real power isn't loud. It's steady.

Real power doesn't dominate. It directs.

Real power doesn't punish to protect ego; it teaches to build character.

You don't win power struggles by overpowering students. You win by not needing to.

Let your calm speak louder than their chaos. Let your clarity outlast their confusion.

And let your *consistency of care* be the loudest presence in the room.

That's how you master the pivot. That's how you lead with lasting impact.

CHAPTER 14

# ASK YOURSELF???
# REFLECT. GROW. REPEAT.

Every year you spend in the classroom should make you better than the year before. If it doesn't, then something's off. This profession isn't meant for standing still. Things change, curriculum, technology, student needs, even the way society talks about learning. If you're going to keep up, you have got to be willing to change, too.

And that starts with questions. Real questions. Tough questions. The kind of questions that make you uncomfortable, because that is where growth lives.

Ask yourself:

- Am I setting my students up for success, or am I preparing them for failure?
- What does "success" actually look like for me? And what might it look like for my students?

Here's the truth...sometimes we are doing what we think is best, when really, we're giving students what we wish we had as kids. That's not always a bad thing, but it can be dangerous if it blinds us to what they actually need right now. Their lives aren't our lives. Their world isn't the one we grew up in.

That's why feedback matters. Not just from administrators or peers, but from your students. Ask them what's working and what's not working. It takes humility, but it also takes courage. Students will tell you things that sting. They'll point out blind spots you didn't know you had. But it is necessary to learn about those blind spots, because that is how you level up.

It's also important to check whether what you're doing is moving your students forward or leaving them stuck. *Are your strategies giving them confidence? Or are they making them feel powerless?* Growth in your classroom won't happen by accident. You need a game plan; not just for the lessons you teach, but also for how you teach those lessons.

And while you're reflecting, be real with yourself. Our shortcomings can slip into our work without us even realizing it. The frustration we feel at home can show up in the way we handle discipline. Old wounds from our childhood can sneak into how we treat students when they remind us of ourselves. That's why reflection is so powerful; it keeps us from repeating cycles we were supposed to break.

We also have to separate "what I think they need" from "what they actually need." Resources matter, but so does listening.

Think about Ms. Daniels, a veteran teacher who was convinced one of her 10th graders, Marcus, needed stricter discipline. He was restless in class, quick to talk back, and always late with assignments. But after sitting down with him and really listening, she learned he was taking care of his little sister every night while his mom worked double shifts. What Marcus needed wasn't more detentions. He needed flexibility in deadlines and a quiet place to work after school. That small shift turned a "problem student" into one of her most consistent workers.

Or take Mr. Greene, a new teacher who thought his students weren't performing well because his grading wasn't tough enough. He doubled down, more tests, more red marks, more zeros for late work. But instead of improving, the class shut down. After getting honest feedback from his students, Mr. Greene realized his students weren't lacking motivation; they were confused about expectations. Once he replaced "gotcha" grading with clear rubrics and consistent feedback, performance improved across the board.

You might believe a student needs more rules when what they need is more trust. You might think they need your version of "success," when what they really need is the space to define it for themselves. Listening changes everything.

Above all...be authentic. Students know when you're pretending.

Ask Ms. Rivera, who started the year trying to mimic the "strict but fair" style of a mentor she admired. The act exhausted her, and her students sensed the disconnect. One day, Ms. Rivera dropped the act. She stopped policing every tiny thing, started telling her own stories, and admitted when she didn't know the answer. Her relationships with her students changed almost overnight. They respected her more because she was real with them.

Teach the value of one voice, one choice, and the consequences that come with it. Remember: you're an educator, not their parent. The line matters. But that doesn't mean you can't care deeply. It means you care in a way that empowers them, not controls them.

When students know your care is authentic, they'll meet you halfway. They will take risks, own their mistakes, and believe you when you say they are capable of more.

When feedback comes your way, take it. Even when it hurts. Accepting correction not only makes you better, it helps you see the power struggles happening inside your students and gives you tools to respond with patience instead of ego.

Finally, don't stop asking questions just because you think you already know the answers. The moment you believe you've "arrived" is the moment you start slipping. True credibility doesn't come from knowing everything. It comes from being willing to learn, no matter how long you've been in the game.

Ask yourself: ***Am I just an educator in the making, or am I an educator willing to make it?***

**SELF-ASSESSMENT** ***(REFLECT AS A PARENT, TEACHER, OR MENTOR)***

1. What was missing in my childhood?
2. What do I wish I had received from a teacher or parent?
3. What evidence do I have that affirms what I'm doing is working?
4. Who is doing this work in a way I admire?
5. In what ways can I improve my practice?
6. How am I tracking my progress?

7. What are my triggers?
8. How do I show up when I'm triggered?
9. Do I ask for feedback? Why or why not?
10. What do I want students to say about me in 5-10 years?

**BONUS:** Am I trying to live through others?

Growth is a cycle; reflect, grow, repeat. The better we get at asking ourselves these questions, the better we get at giving our students what they truly need.

In the end, this work has never been just about lesson plans or test scores. It's about legacy. Every decision we make in the classroom shapes a story that will be told long after the last bell rings. The questions we ask ourselves today are the seeds for the kind of educators and human beings we will become tomorrow. Keep planting with purpose. Keep growing with courage. And remember: when we rise, our students rise with us.

# SELF-ASSESSMENT

Reflect as a parent, teacher, or mentor

| # | QUESTION | THOUGHT STARTER |
|---|---|---|
| 1 | What was missing in my childhood? | Identify gaps in your early experiences that may influence how you lead, teach, or respond today. |
| 2 | What do I wish I had received from a teacher or parent? | Think about the support, guidance, or encouragement you needed and how you can now provide it. |
| 3 | What evidence do I have that affirms what I'm doing is working? | Look for real outcomes, not assumptions. What proof shows your impact is effective? |
| 4 | Who is doing this work in a way I admire? | Consider role models who demonstrate the standard you want to reach. What specifically stands out? |
| 5 | In what ways can I improve my practice? | Be honest about areas of growth. Where can you become more intentional, consistent, or effective? |
| 6 | How am I tracking my progress? | Growth requires measurement. How are you monitoring improvement over time? |
| 7 | What are my triggers? | Recognize the moments, behaviors, or situations that cause emotional reactions. |
| 8 | How do I show up when I'm triggered? | Reflect on your behavior under pressure. Are your responses aligned with your values? |
| 9 | Do I ask for feedback? Why or why not? | Evaluate your openness to growth. Are you seeking input or avoiding accountability? |
| 10 | What do I want students to say about me in 5–10 years? | Define your long-term impact. What legacy are you intentionally creating? |
| ★ | Bonus: Am I trying to live through others? | Check your motives. Are you guiding others, or projecting your own unmet goals onto them? |

**Clarity creates growth. Growth creates impact.**

EPILOGUE

# OUR STORY
# A LEGACY OF INFLUENCE

Our story isn't just mine. It's yours. It's ours. Every lesson, every win, every loss, every moment in the hallway with a student who needed a second chance, it's all part of the same fabric we've been stitching together since the first page. If you've been here from the start, you know this book wasn't written for comfort. It was written to stir you. To make you look at the way you move in this work we do and ask, *"Am I really making the impact I think I am?"*

In the educational context, effectiveness can be defined as achieving desired learning outcomes, fostering critical thinking, and promoting holistic development. Teachers who wield their influence effectively create environments where students feel valued and inspired to participate actively in their learning. By sharing your passion for the subject and demonstrating relatable connections, educators can significantly enhance students' motivation and engagement. Shifting away from a control mindset allows educators to embrace student autonomy and agency in the learning process. The shift from control to influence cultivates lifelong learners who are motivated to explore, inquire, and innovate beyond the classroom walls. When students learn in environments that prioritize influence, they develop critical thinking skills and an appreciation for collaboration and essential skills for navigating an ever-changing world. Exploring the statements "Influence impacts effectiveness" and "Forget about control" within education illuminates a progressive philosophy that emphasizes collaboration, student agency, and meaningful relationships. This approach not only enhances teaching and learning outcomes but also nurtures a generation of empowered individuals who are equipped to succeed in diverse contexts. By embracing the power of influence and moving away from control, educators can create transformative learning experiences that resonate deeply with students, preparing them for their future roles as active and engaged adults.

I've learned from great coaches who poured into me like water into dry soil. I've learned from horrible coaches who left cracks in the ground. Cracks I had to learn how to fill. I've been humbled by the brilliance of my students, their questions hitting me like chalk dust in sunlight, floating until they landed somewhere deep. I've been sharpened by mentoring other educators, watching them turn that "first-year fire" into a steady, lasting flame. And I've tripped over my own mistakes; sometimes hard enough to leave a scar that still itches when the lesson comes back around.

One of my former coaches/mentors, and now a good friend, LSR once shared a line attributed to John Dewey: *"We don't learn from experience; we learn from reflecting on experience".* The caveat is, only if we desire to. That's the heartbeat of your opportunity gifted within these pages. It's not enough to just be here. We've got to be awake while we're here. We've got to examine what we're doing, why we're doing it, and who it's truly serving.

This book was written to examine your approach to the work.

This book was written to pressure-test your beliefs.

This book was written to encourage you to stay the course and to course-correct when you're drifting.

My mother, Gloria Newsome, had a way of boiling down life to its purest truth: *"You are either helping or hurting the situation. There is no middle."*

That's as real as it gets. Tap in. Level up. Do whatever it takes to be on the right side of impact and influence. The only thing you truly control is you: your choices, your words, your energy, your decisions. If you've been coasting, wake up. If you've been hiding behind excuses, step forward. If you've been pouring into others but forgetting yourself, get whole again. That's your legacy. That's our story. And it's still being written in every classroom, every conversation, every act of influence from here on out.

# Ī BĒFORE Ē

INFLUENCE AND IMPACT LEAD TO LONG-TERM EFFECTIVENESS. FORGET ABOUT CONTROL.

www.ingramcontent.com/pod-product-compliance
Lightning Source LLC
LaVergne TN
LVHW081318110826
845149LV00006B/1542
* 9 7 9 8 9 9 5 0 9 1 2 0 2 *